THE HOLY SPIRIT

His Person and Work

by

EDWARD HENRY BICKERSTETH

Companion volume to "THE TRINITY"

KREGEL PUBLICATIONS
Grand Rapids, Michigan 49501

Library of Congress Catalog Card Number 59-13640
ISBN 0-8254-2227-2

The Holy Spirit, His Person and Work by Edward Henry Bickersteth
was originally published under the title, *The Spirit of Life.* This
edition, complete and unabridged, published by Kregel Publications,
a division of Kregel, Inc., P.O. Box 2607, Grand Rapids, Michigan
49501. All rights reserved.

Reprint Edition 1959
Second Printing .1967
Third Printing 1973
New Paperback Edition 1976

FOREWORD

Satan is occupied with two great enterprises. The first of these given his careful attention is intended to keep the sinner away from the Saviour. He knows that if the sinner once reaches the side of the wounded Man of Calvary in faith and trust, then he has lost another member of his host to the family of God. His second great work is to prevent the Christian from making the Holy Spirit the Lord of his life. He knows quite well that the believer in Christ Jesus who makes the Holy Spirit his Lord will become an active and intelligent servant of God who will attack his kingdom successfully.

When one trusts the Saviour with his heart and soul, then his *soul* is saved. When one makes the Holy Spirit his Lord, and trusts his life to that wonderful Person, then his *life* is saved. Because of these two great facts Bishop Bickersteth wrote his wonderful book THE TRINITY (Kregel's), and also this present volume. These books will make the Christian an effective servant of God. He will have the power necessary for fruitful service. He will have such a knowledge of God as will preserve him from false doctrines and from fruitless living.

These messages have profoundly influenced my own life and ministry. I commend this volume to God's people of every denomination. You will be inspired, enriched and enlightened as you read it.

WALTER LEWIS WILSON, M.D., D.D., L.H.D.

PREFACE

SOME years since it was permitted me to write a treatise entitled " The Rock of Ages," on the One Eternal Godhead of the Father, and of the Son, and of the Holy Ghost. The book was adopted by the Religious Tract Society, and has been widely circulated in England and America: it has also been translated into German: and I have received most grateful assurances from many anxious enquirers after truth, that the testimony of Scripture set forth in that work has, through God's infinite mercy, led them to the Saviour's feet. The communications which have reached me on this subject, some of them sent to me from dying beds, and others from the bosom of home life, may not be made public, but they lie deep in my heart, among the choicest and most cherished memories of my ministry. I may, however, mention that the book has been used as a class-book, not only in schools at home, but also among the native catechists of Hindûstan, and by brethren engaged in missions to the Jews. That God should deign to use so humble an instrument in the promotion of his kingdom is only another proof how sometimes he is pleased to choose the things which are not to bring to nought things which are.

There was one chapter in that treatise, which was designed to establish the proposition, *That Scripture in the Old and New Testament alike proves the co-equal Godhead of the Father, and of the Son, and of the Holy Ghost.* But it was of course impossible in a chapter, which only extended to twenty-five pages, to enter at any length into the Scripture testimony regarding the Spirit's Divine operations. I could do little more than barely indicate the evidences, which might be gathered from every field of his manifold work, to his Personality and Godhead. These evidences, enlarged and expanded, are embodied in the work now presented to the reader.* And in addition I have sought (humbly and reverently I trust, remembering how great a mystery is here treated of) to enquire what is the teaching of the word of God with respect to the Spirit's infinite unction of the Son of Man, to His inspiration of Holy Scripture, to His striving with the world, to His quickening of those dead in sins, to His progressive sanctification of those who are quickened, and finally with respect to the issue of His work

---

* Where the words, employed in the chapter alluded to above, expressed my meaning more clearly than any others which I could command, I have not scrupled to repeat them. And the same remark refers to the quotations I have made from my "Commentary on the New Testament" on some of the leading Scriptures which treat of the Holy Spirit's work, especially John iii. 1—16 ; xvi. 7—11 ; and Rom. vii. 14, to viii. 17.

in the everlasting kingdom of our Lord and Saviour
Jesus Christ. So that this treatise may be in some
measure regarded as the supplement and complement
of the former.

My object in this later as in that earlier essay has
been to present the witness of Holy Writ in its sim-
plicity and power, when spiritual things are compared
with spiritual. And I would therefore beg the reader
not to expect here any learned disquisitions on abstruse
points, nor even critical investigations further than are
necessary to establish the plain meaning of the passages
adduced. My hope is that teachers in our schools,
and missionaries to Christ's poor, and possibly evangelists and pastors, may find in these pages a repertory
of Scripture proofs to which they can easily refer for
at least the leading subjects of this great and exhaustless theme.

From the blessed Reformation to our own day, the
Church of Christ has had many times of refreshing
from the presence of her Lord. There have been many
and marked effusions of the Divine Spirit. But the
very abundance of the grace vouchsafed has often
seemed to tempt the enemy to produce transient but
specious counterfeits of the Spirit's holy and abiding
operations, and has rendered the necessity the greater
of distinguishing between emotional excitement and
transforming grace. It would have been foreign to
the character of this treatise to enter into any discussion
of what are commonly called " Revivals of Religion."
Perhaps there have been few such revivals, in which

there has not been something of God's work which is and must be ever true and lasting, and something of man's work which is fruitless and evanescent. But, although the subject is not discussed, I venture to hope that there are plain Scriptural criteria and texts given in this work (especially in chapters vi., vii., and viii.), by which that which is born of the flesh may be distinguished from that which is born of the Spirit.

May He only vouchsafe his blessing who has promised, " As the rain cometh down and the snow from heaven and returneth not thither, but watereth the earth and causeth it to bring forth and bud,—so shall my word be that goeth forth out of my mouth, it shall not return to me void " (Isa. lv. 10), and in the great harvest field some sheaves of precious grain shall be gathered from this humble effort to sow the incorruptible seed of life.

E. H. B.

CHRIST CHURCH VICARAGE, HAMPSTEAD :

SUMMARY OF ARGUMENT

Chapter I. The Witness of Scripture:

> That of the Old Testament, in the Pentateuch and the book of
> Job, in the historical books, in the Psalms, and in the
> Prophets : it is a progressive revelation :
> That of the New Testament, in the Gospels, in the Acts, in the
> Epistles, in the Apocalypse : this likewise progressive.
>
> pp. 13–36.

Chapter II. The Distinct Personality of the Holy
Spirit :

> Not to be confounded with the Father or the Son, for Scripture
> reveals the simultaneous co-operation and manifestation of
> Three Infinite Agents :
> Sometimes the term Spirit is used to signify the gifts or graces
> of the Spirit : this does not disprove the Personality of the
> Holy Ghost ; for, according to the Scriptures,
> He possesses such qualities as a person only can possess. He
> performs such actions as a person only can perform. He is
> capable of suffering such injuries as a person only can suffer.
> He is designated by masculine pronouns, though the noun
> Spirit is neuter.
>
> pp. 37–49.

Chapter III. The Eternal Godhead of the Holy
Spirit :

> His attributes are the attributes of Godhead.
> His acts are the actings of Godhead.
> He is regarded and spoken of, as God, in Holy Writ.
> He is associated with the Father and the Son in glory and
> worship.
>
> pp. 50–70.

Even in the case of those who finally repulse His grace
  He may enlighten the understanding;
  He may work strong convictions;
  He may invite them to embrace the Gospel;
  He may warn them and awaken alarm;
  He may wound the heart by His word;
  He may persuade them to effect an outward reformation.
Examples in Scripture of those convicted but not converted.
The Spirit may be grieved, vexed, insulted, blasphemed.
Blasphemy of the Spirit, and the sin unto death.

pp. 104–119.

CHAPTER VII.   THE HOLY SPIRIT QUICKENING THE SOUL
  TO LIFE:

The conversation of our Lord with Nicodemus:
Scripture designations for the new birth of the soul:
The Spirit's illumination of the understanding:
His saving conviction of sin, righteousness, and judgment:
He brings the soul to self-despair and self-surrender:
He enables the contrite heart to pray:
He effectuates the obedience of faith:
He gives peace with God:
He sheds abroad the love of God in the heart:
He awakens godly sorrow:
He leads the convert to confess Christ.

pp. 120–139.

CHAPTER VIII.   THE HOLY SPIRIT SANCTIFYING THE
  BELIEVER:

Definition of sanctification: it is progressive.
Sanctification of the believer includes—
  An ever-deepening knowledge of the things of God,
  A growing delight in the heavenly duties of prayer and
    praise,
  A more and more vigorous faith in the salvation of Christ,
  A more entire submission of our will to the will of God,
  A more resolute crucifying of the flesh and a more earnest
    cultivation of the fruits of the Spirit,

A readier willingness to serve and suffer for our Master here,
And a brighter prospect of reigning with Him for ever.
On declensions and falls : the Holy Spirit restoring the soul.
The seal of the Spirit.

CHAPTER IX.   THE ISSUE OF THE HOLY SPIRIT'S WORK—

In the everlasting kingdom,
In the perfection of the glorified saint,
In the completion of the Elect Church,
In the new heavens and the new earth wherein dwelleth righteousness.

CHAPTER I

"THE words of God are to theology what the facts
of nature are to science: they may not be set aside by
reasoning: whether we can harmonize them or not,
they claim the obedience of faith." Let me apply the
axiom, thus happily expressed by a deep thinker, to
the momentous theme with which my treatise proposes
to deal. And to this end let me first gather together,
though I must indicate some of them by reference only,
all the scattered notices of Holy Writ regarding the
Divine Spirit, before I attempt to establish that
Catholic doctrine which, I am well assured, can alone
stand the test of this great principle. These will be
the data of my argument. In this preliminary stage
I shall not do more than endeavour to bring forward
the statements of Scripture in their plain grammatical
meaning, for the most part observing the historical
order in which they stand. And yet even in thus
digging the foundation, I would remind myself and my
readers that it is the groundwork of that temple in which
the ark of the covenant is set, and that the labourer
herein especially needs a restrained footstep and a
reverent hand. When we search the Scriptures we

draw nigh unto God. And this, which is true of all inquiry into these living oracles, is pre-eminently true of those which reveal the presence and the power of the Holy Spirit. For we cannot and we would not forget the solemn warning of our Lord, "Whosoever speaketh a word against the Son of man, it shall be forgiven him; but whosoever speaketh against the Holy Ghost, it shall not be forgiven him, neither in

Matt. xii. 32. this world, neither in the world to come." May He enable us to keep our foot, remembering that the place whereon we stand is holy ground.

No one can read the Old and New Testaments without being aware of the indications of a mighty mysterious Being, called the Spirit of God, or the Spirit of Jehovah, continually occurrent in the work of creation and Providence, and especially apparent in the more eventful crises of the Church's history. It remains for those who presume to affirm that the unity of the Godhead is so simple as to preclude any plurality of Persons subsisting therein, to explain WHO this Being is. These indications meet us from Genesis to Revelation.

Thus, no sooner is the fact of the original creation of all things by God, and the formless and void state of our earth before the work of the first day, revealed, than we meet with the remarkable words, "The Spirit of God moved (מְרַחֶפֶת) on the face of the waters." The Hebrew word implies the tremulous fluttering or brooding of a bird over its nest, infusing life from its own vital warmth. So Milton, in his invocation of the

Gen. i. 2. Spirit, writes :—

> "Thou from the first
> Wast present, and with mighty wings outspread,
> Dovelike satest brooding on the vast abyss,
> And madest it pregnant."
>
> *Paradise Lost*, book i., 19—22.

Our thoughts are here directed to the Holy Spirit as the quickening Creator from the beginning. And even before the foundations of our world were laid, there are Scriptures which testify that he was the Fashioner of other worlds and the Author of life to other intelligences. Thus, in one of the earliest books of inspiration, we not only have the assertion from the lips of Elihu, "The Spirit of God hath made me," but find the remarkable testimony of the patriarch Job in the midst of his appeal to the works of the Great Creator—"By His Spirit he hath garnished the heavens." And to this agree the words of the Psalmist, who not only says of man and the living creatures of the earth, "Thou sendest forth thy Spirit; they are created;" but in language, suggestive (to say no more) of the deepest mystery of our faith, affirms, "By the Word of Jehovah were the heavens made and all the host of them by the Spirit of his mouth." Job xxvi. 13: xxxiii. 4.

Psa. civ. 30; xxxiii. 6.

The next great epoch in the world's history was that of the flood. And to pass over the fact that Enoch was one of those holy prophets which have been since the world began, who spake as they were moved by the Holy Ghost; this was the first utterance of judgment impending over a guilty world. Jehovah said, "My Spirit shall not always strive with man for that he also is flesh : yet his days shall be an hundred and twenty years." Jude 14; Luke i. 70; 2 Pet. i. 21

Gen. vi. 3.

Again, only noting, as we pass on, that Abraham, the father of the faithful, is declared by God to be " a prophet," and that, when Joseph in God's name foretold the future, this was the irresistible conclusion forced upon the mind of Pharaoh, " Can we find such a one as this is, a man in whom the Spirit of God is ?" let us come to the legal dispensation. Gen. xx. 7.

Gen. xli. 38.

When Moses, overborne by the ingratitude and unbelief of Israel, complained, " I am not able to bear all this people alone, because it is too heavy for me," we learn in WHOSE might he had hitherto sustained the load of a nation's jurisprudence and governance. " The Lord said unto Moses, Gather unto me seventy men of the elders of Israel . . . and I will take of the Spirit which is upon thee, and will put it upon them." And so we read, " It came to pass, that when the Spirit rested upon them, they prophesied and did not cease. But there remained two of the men in the camp, the name of the one was Eldad, and the name of the other Medad, and the Spirit rested upon them . . . and they prophesied in the camp." And when Joshua, jealous for his master's honour, exclaimed, " My lord Moses forbid them," Moses answered, " Enviest thou for my sake ? Would God that all the Lord's people were prophets, and that the Lord would put his Spirit upon them." This incident speaks volumes, and was in itself a wondrous anticipation of that baptism of the Spirit which is the especial prerogative of the incarnate Son of God.   Nor can we forget that even the inferior work of constructing and furnishing the material sanctuary was only intrusted to one of whom the Lord spake unto Moses, saying, " See, I have called by name Bezaleel, . . and I have filled him with the Spirit of God in wisdom and in understanding and in knowledge and in all manner of workmanship." Again when it pleased the Lord to bless Israel by the lips of a false prophet, that the glory of the benediction might be more conspicuously of God and not of man, we read, " Balaam saw Israel abiding in his tents according to their tribes, and the Spirit of God came upon him, and he took up his parable." Other Scriptures tell us that " God gave his Good Spirit to instruct " his people in the wilder-

Numb. xi. 10
—30.

Exod. xxxi.
2, 3, and
xxxv. 30,
31.

Num. xxiv.
2, 3.
Nehem. ix.
19, 20.

ness, and that it was the Spirit of Jehovah who caused
them to rest.   And when Moses was to be gathered Isa. lxiii. 14.
to his fathers, this was the emphatic qualification of his
successor, "Take thee Joshua, the son of Nun, a man
in whom is the Spirit, and lay thine hand upon him." Num. xxvii.
And so it was: "Joshua the son of Nun was full of 18.
the Spirit of wisdom, for Moses had laid his hands upon
him."   Thus, from Egypt to Canaan was Israel under Deut. xxxiv.
the guidance of the Eternal Spirit. 9.

In the times of the Judges his presence is equally
apparent.   Thus of Othniel we read, "When the
children of Israel cried unto the Lord, the Lord raised
up a deliverer who delivered them, even Othniel the
son of Kenaz, Caleb's younger brother; and the Spirit
of the Lord came (*Heb.* "was") upon him, and he
judged Israel and went out to war."   Of Gideon, that Judg. iii. 10.
princely warrior, it is written, "The Spirit of the Lord
came upon (*Heb.* "clothed") Gideon, and he blew a
trumpet, and Abi-ezer was gathered after him."   So ch. vi. 34.
likewise of Jephthah.   And of Samson, we have no ch. xi. 29.
less than four distinct intimations in whose strength
he wrought his mighty works, even the strength of ch. xiii. 25;
the Omnipotent Spirit of Jehovah. xiv. 6, 19;
xv. 14.

Let us come to the kings of Israel.   While their
first anointed monarch kept the covenant of his God, the
Spirit of the Lord enabled him to discharge all his prophetical, military, and royal duties.   But when he for- 1 Sam. xi. 6,
sook the path of obedience, this marks the fatal epoch 10 : xi. 6.
of his history : "The Spirit of the Lord departed from
Saul," though he once again vouchsafed to show in
him and his servants the miraculous sign of prophecy. 1 Sam. xvi.
His sun set in darkness.   But of David, on the other 14 ; xix. 20,
22.
hand, we read, when Samuel took the horn of oil and
anointed him in the midst of his brethren, "The
Spirit of the Lord came upon David from that day for-

CHAP. I.

1 Sam. xvi. 13. ward." In his presence he walked, for he asks,
Psa. cxxxix. "Whither shall I go from thy Spirit?" On his guid-
7.
ance he depended, for he prays, "Thy Spirit is good:
Psa. cxliii. 10. lead me." To his influence he owed the allegiance of
1 Chron. xii. the armies of Israel. This, in the hour of his broken-
18.
hearted penitence, was the burden of his grief: "Take
not thy Holy Spirit from me: restore unto me the
Psa. li. 11, 12. joy of thy salvation, and uphold me with thy free
Spirit." But God took not his mercy from him.
"By the Spirit" he revealed to him the pattern of
1 Chron. that temple which Solomon was to build. And
xxviii. 12.
among the last words of David, words which tell
whence came all the heavenly inspiration of the sweet
Psalmist of Israel, it is recorded, "The Spirit of the
2 Sam. xxiii. Lord spake by me and his word was in my tongue."
2.
And when he was gathered to his fathers, this was the
message which his son was inspired to place in the
forefront of those proverbs of Divine wisdom which
have been the heritage of every age. "Turn you at
my reproof: behold I will pour out my Spirit unto
Prov. i. 23. you, I will make known my words unto you."

After the great defeat of the Ethiopian armies by
Asa, we read that it was by the direct inspiration of
the Spirit of God that the prophet Azariah the son
of Oded went out to meet the royal victor on his return
to Jerusalem and renewed and ratified the covenant
betwixt the tribes of Judah and Benjamin and their
2 Chron. xv. God.
1—8.
We now arrive at the golden age of prophecy. And
speaking first of him who was the chosen representative
of that goodly fellowship, Elijah, how incidental but
how suggestive are the words of Obadiah as revealing
the secret of the prophet's majestic and mysterious
power, "The Spirit of the Lord shall carry thee
1 Kings xviii. whither I know not." So Zedekiah's sarcastic question
12.

as he struck Micaiah on the cheek, yet shows the inspiration accorded by all to every prophet, " Which way went the Spirit of the Lord from me to speak unto thee?" And when Elijah's mantle was to fall on his successor, this was Elisha's prayer, " Let a double portion of thy Spirit be upon me." When Jordan was parted before him, this was the confession of the sons of the prophets, " The Spirit of Elijah doth rest on Elisha:" and when they would seek for his master and theirs, this was the plea they instinctively urged, " Peradventure the Spirit of the Lord hath taken him up and cast him upon some mountain, or into some valley." So entirely were the prophets esteemed to be under the guidance and governance of the Holy Ghost.

1 Kings xxii. 24.

2 Kings ii. 9, 15, 16.

In another most eventful crisis of the history of Judah, when the swarming multitudes of Moab and Ammon came up to destroy Jerusalem, and Jehoshaphat prayed, " O our God, wilt thou not judge them? for we have no might against this great company that cometh against us; neither know we what to do: but our eyes are upon thee,"—then, in the sight of all Judah standing before the Lord with their little ones, their wives, and their children—" upon Jahaziel, a Levite of the sons of Asaph, came the Spirit of the Lord in the midst of the congregation, and he said, Thus saith the Lord unto you, Be not afraid nor dismayed by reason of this great multitude, for the battle is not yours, but God's." The voice was recognised as Jehovah's; and we read, " Jehoshaphat bowed his head with his face to the ground: and all Judah and the inhabitants of Jerusalem fell before the Lord, worshipping the Lord."

2 Chron. xx. 12—18.

And when the king and the princes of Judah left the

house of the Lord God of their fathers and served groves and idols, when the Lord sent prophets unto them to testify against them and they would not give ear; then we read, " The Spirit of God came upon (*Heb.* "clothed") Zechariah the son of Jehoiada the priest, which stood above the people, and said unto them, Thus saith God, Why transgress ye the commandments of the Lord, that ye cannot prosper? because ye have forsaken the Lord, he hath also forsaken you. And they conspired against him and stoned him with stones at the commandment of the king in the court of the house of the Lord. And when he died he said, The Lord look 2 Chron. xxiv. upon it and require it." A peculiar interest attaches
20—22. to this closing testimony of Zechariah, thus sealed with his blood, from his being in all probability the one alluded to by our Lord as Zacharias the son of Barachias in his last prophetic woes pronounced upon Matt. xxiii. Jerusalem. Jehoiada was most likely also called Bara-
35. chiah. It was not unfrequent to have a second name, especially when that of Jehovah formed part of the first. And the books of the Chronicles being regarded as the conclusion of the *historical canon* of the Old Testament, our Lord in citing the history of the martyrdom of Zacharias from that book, and in going backward from it to the martyrdom of Abel, comprises all Jewish history (though chronologically the death of Jer. xxvi. 23. Urijah was·later), and combines the acts and sufferings of all the martyrs whose blood cried from the ground against Jerusalem. The record in Chronicles assures us that it was " clothed" in the strength of the Holy Ghost that Zechariah thus witnessed and suffered and died.

And now let us group together the utterances of the great evangelical prophet, Isaiah, regarding the work

of the Divine Spirit. Looking on to the future re-
storation of Israel, he foresees that time of blessedness,
" When the Lord shall have washed away the filth of
the daughters of Zion, and shall have purged the blood
of Jerusalem by the Spirit of judgment and by the
Spirit of burning." What is this but the plenary ac- Isa. iv. 4;
xxviii. 6.
complishment to Israel of that baptism of fire, which
the voice in the wilderness proclaimed ? Again, having
foretold the birth of Messiah, the virgin-born Em-
manuel, the Prince of Peace, the rod out of the stem of
Jesse, he describes the unction of the Holy Ghost
which should abide upon him without measure. " The
Spirit of the Lord shall rest upon him, the Spirit of
wisdom and understanding, the Spirit of counsel and
might, the Spirit of knowledge and of the fear of the
Lord, and shall make him of quick understanding in
the fear of the Lord." Again, when the rebellious ch. xi. 2, 3.
children are warned, this is noted as their crowning sin,
" They cover with a covering but not of my Spirit,
saith the Lord." Again, when the desolations of Zion ch. xxx. 1.
are foretold, they are to last, " until the Spirit be
poured out upon us from on high," whereas the birds
of prey brood over Idumæa, for " the Spirit of the
Lord hath gathered them." And in that magnificent ch. xxxii. 15,
& xxxiv.
16.
prophecy which extends through the last twenty-seven
chapters of this book, how frequently does the power
of the Divine Spirit appear. In his hands are the
issues of life and death. His are the grandest works ch. xl. 7.
of creation. With him the Eternal Father anoints ch. xl. 12, 13.
Messiah. By him he waters and revives his Church. ch. xlii. 1.
ch. xliv. 3.
He with the Father sends forth the Son. He with- ch. xlviii. 16.
stands all the pride of the foe, and abides with his
own for ever. He rests on the Saviour in his Divine ch. lix. 19, 21.
embassy of mercy. And in the solemn retrospect of ch. lxi. 1.

God's dealings with Israel, he it was whom they vexed with their ingratitude, he who dwelt in them as in his temple, he who brought them safely through the wilderness to the promised rest of Canaan.

Isa. lxiii. 10, 11, 14.

The prophet Jeremiah does not name the Spirit of God, though he dwells upon his especial office of writing the Divine law upon the heart. But when we come to the sublime grandeur of Ezekiel, it is the Spirit who animates the fourfold cherubim and their mystic wheels: it is the Spirit who entered into the prophet and set him on his feet, and lifted him up betwixt the earth and heaven, and brought him in a vision to Chaldea, and said unto him, "Speak, Thus saith the Lord:" it is the Spirit who is promised to recreate the heart of man, and to breathe life into the lifeless slain in the vision of the valley of dry bones. And this is Ezekiel's closing message before the gorgeous vision of the temple is recorded, "Neither will I hide my face any more from them: for I have poured my Spirit upon the house of Israel, saith the Lord God."

Compare Jer. xxxi. 33, with 2 Cor. iii. 3.

Ezek. i. 12, 20, 21, and x. 17.

chs. ii 2; iii. 12, 14—24; viii. 3; xi. 1, 5, 24; xxxvii. 1; xliii. 5.

chs. xi. 19; xviii. 31; xxxvi. 26, 27; and xxxvii. 9, 14.

ch. xxxix. 29.

Daniel's saintly wisdom was such that it wrung the confession alike from Nebuchadnezzar and Belshazzar that "the Spirit of the holy gods" was in him; and he was commissioned to record the promised unction of the Most Holy, and the advent and atoning death of the Divine Anointed One. Joel is inspired to foretell the Pentecostal effusion of the Spirit. Micah asks in victorious faith, "Is the Spirit of the Lord straitened?" and declares for the execution of his embassy, "I am full of power by the Spirit of the Lord." And when Israel was restored from Babylon, this in their weakness was declared to be the secret of their strength. "So my Spirit remaineth among you, fear ye not:"

Dan. iv. 8, 9, 18; v. 11, 14.

ch. ix. 24—26.

Joel ii. 28, 29.

Mic. ii. 7; iii. 8; and compare Neh. ix. 30.

Hag. ii. 5.

in dependence on his secret but omnipotent aid the second temple was to be built, even from the base to the headstone thereof: this resistance of the Spirit was the sin of their fathers: and this is still the hope laid up for Israel, " I will pour upon the house of David and upon the inhabitants of Jerusalem the Spirit of grace and of supplications." And Malachi, who closes the canon of the Old Testament, assures us God " had yet the residue of the Spirit," for his people. Thus even before the evangelical effusion of the Holy Ghost, we have under the elder covenant more than eighty distinct notices of the presence and the power of the One Eternal Spirit.

It is an interesting question whether we can trace any progressive revelation of the work of the Divine Spirit in the Old Testament. I cannot but think that such will reward the search of the patient student. Thus in the Pentateuch and the book of Job we have especially his creative and legislative power revealed; in the historical books his clothing the warriors of Israel with might, his anointing the kings of Israel for their regal administrations, and his endowment of the earlier prophets with miraculous gifts; in the Psalms his deeper subjective work in the heart of man, recreating, restoring, consoling; in Isaiah, evangelical prospects; in Ezekiel, heavenly mysteries; in Daniel, the anointing of Messiah for his atoning sacrifice; in Joel, the promise of the Pentecostal effusion; and in Zechariah, the preintimations of millennial glories.

This, however, was but the glow in the eastern sky before the Sun of righteousness arose with healing in his wings. Our Lord's incarnation by the Holy Ghost of the Virgin Mary was foreannounced by Gabriel to his mother, and was reported by him or another angel to Joseph. Elizabeth, when Mary visited her, spoke

Zech. iv. 6—14.
ch. vii. 12.

ch. xii. 10.

Mal. ii. 15.

Luke i. 35.
Matt. i. 18, 20.

24 *The Witness of Scripture*

Luke i. 15, 41, 67.

out her joy under the inspiration of the same Spirit: so likewise did Zacharias, the father of him who, as our Lord's forerunner, was himself filled with the Holy Ghost even from his mother's womb. On the aged Simeon the Spirit rested and revealed to him Messiah's birth, and prompted his visit to the temple at the very

ch ii. 26, 27.

hour of the presentation there of the Holy Child. And when the time was fulfilled and John came preaching in the wilderness, this was the solemn climax of his prophetic embassy, " He that cometh after me is mightier than I, whose shoes I am not worthy to bear; he shall baptize you with the Holy

Matt. iii. 11; Mark i. 8; Luke iii. 16; John i. 33.

Ghost and with fire."

Upon the manifestation of the Spirit in our Lord's ministry my words must here be very few, as I hope to dwell more at length upon it afterwards. Let it suffice now to say, the descent of the Holy Ghost in a bodily shape like a dove upon him at his baptism was his

Matt. iii. 16, 17; Mark i. 10, 11; Luke iii. 21, 22.

inauguration to the prophetical office; and certified John that he who was thus baptized with the Spirit was himself the predicted Baptizer with the Holy Ghost, the Christ unto whom the Father gives the

John i. 32, 33, and iii. 34.

Spirit without measure. By this Spirit he was led into

Matt. iv. 1; Mark i. 12; Luke iv. 1.

the wilderness to be tempted; and he returned, full of the Spirit, to preach the gospel of the kingdom. The

Luke iv. 14, 18, 22.

new birth of the Spirit was declared by him to be the

John iii. 6–8.

essential mark of discipleship. This was the great gift

Compare Matt. vii. 11, with Luke xi. 13.

for which he taught his followers to pray. This was the power of the utterance he promised them. This

Matt. x. 20; Mark xiii. 11; Luke xii. 12.

was the might in which he wrought his miracles.

Matt. xii. 28.

Against blasphemy of this Spirit he uttered his most

Matt. xii. 31, 32; Mark iii. 29; Luke xii. 10.

solemn warnings. The meekness he required was the meekness of the Holy Ghost.* His great proclamation

Luke ix. 55.

* Luke ix. 55, " *Ye know not what manner of Spirit ye are of,*" *i. e.,* Ye know not that the Spirit of the gospel dispensation

on the last day of the feast was none other than the
offer of the Holy Spirit to all who would come to him. John vii. 37
To the Holy Spirit he ascribed the inspiration of the —39.
oracles of God. This was that other Comforter, the Matt. xxii.
Spirit of truth who proceedeth from the Father, and 43; Mark
whom the Father would send in his name to abide xii. 36.
with them for ever, of whom he spoke such wonderful
words, the same night in which he was betrayed. John xiv. 16,
Anointed with this Spirit he laid down his life that he 17, 26; xv.
might take it again. In that Triune Name, in which —14.
he commanded his apostles to baptize, the Holy Spirit ch. x. 17, 18;
appears as one with the Father and himself in the Heb. ix.14;
Eternal Godhead. And this ere he led them forth to Rom. viii.
Olivet was his parting benediction, "Behold I send 11.
the promise of my Father upon you; but tarry ye in Matt. xxviii.
the city of Jerusalem, until ye be endued with power 19.
from on high." Luke xxiv.
49.

The book of the Acts, or as it has been not inaptly
called *the Gospel of the Spirit,* takes up the latest
threads of the narrative in Luke, tells us that it was
through the Holy Ghost our risen Lord gave commandment to the apostles in the forty days which intervened betwixt his resurrection and ascension, and
records with greater precision the promise of the baptism of the Spirit. Here we learn how Peter, like his Acts i. 2, 5, 8.
Master, received the written word as the voice of the
Holy Ghost. Here the glories of the first Pentecost ch. i. 16.
of the Christian Church are fully described.* Peter ch. ii. 1—47.

---

is a gentle, forbearing, dovelike Spirit. Such is the Spirit ye see
in me. Such is the Spirit I have given you for your ministry.
This is the day of grace, and the time of long-suffering and
patient love.

* It would be foreign to the practical character of this treatise
to discuss at any length the nature of the gift of tongues; but I
may state my own deliberate conviction, that when we read that

answers the Sanhedrim, "filled with the Holy Ghost," and he and John having returned to their company and having prayed, "the place was shaken, where they were assembled together; and they were all filled with the Holy Ghost and spake the word of God with boldness. Here the awful majesty of the Divine Spirit is vindicated in the death of Ananias and Sapphira. The Holy Spirit is represented as witnessing of Christ's exaltation, as qualifying the deacons for their diaconate; as enabling the protomartyr Stephen for his ministry and anointing him for his death; as testifying to the reality of Philip's work at Samaria; as directing the evangelist to the eunuch, and catching him away when his message of life was spoken; as filling that chosen vessel of mercy, Saul of Tarsus; as edifying and comforting the Church; as commanding Peter to preach the gospel to Cornelius and his house, and owning the

Acts iv. 8, 31.

ch. v. 1—11.

ch. v. 32.
ch. vi. 3.

ch. vi. 5, 10;
vii. 51, 55.
ch. viii. 15—
17.

ch. viii. 29,
39.
ch. ix. 17.
ch. ix. 31.

---

ch. ii. 4.

the disciples in the day of Pentecost "began to speak with other tongues (ἐτέραις γλώσσαις) as the Spirit gave them utterance." He enabled them to speak in divers human languages, the languages of the nations of the Roman world, languages which, as Galilean peasants, they had never learned, but in which the Holy Ghost then empowered them to express with perfect facility the wonderful works of God. It was a miracle which, perhaps more than any other, speaks of the human mind brought into immediate contact with the Divine mind. This miracle qualified unlettered disciples to preach the gospel to every nation under heaven, and in their case repaired the ruin which the confusion of tongues at Babel had wrought. No theory which would explain this speaking with tongues to consist of inarticulate utterances, or of aught except intelligible human languages, will, as it seems to me, stand the light of Scripture or the testimony of antiquity. "The apostles were gifted with the tongues of all nations, because Christ sent them to preach to all nations." And this miraculous gift seems only to have been vouchsafed during the apostolic age, and to have ceased with the completion of the canon of the New Testament.

Chrysostom, quoted by Wordsworth.

word spoken with manifest tokens of his presence, a transparent proof which convinced all gainsayers that God had opened the gate of life to the Gentiles; and as empowering Barnabas to confirm those who believed at Antioch, and revealing to Agabus the great dearth which was to come upon the Roman world. Further- more we see how distinctly the first apostles to the Gentiles were sent forth under his Divine superintend- ance; for it is written, " As certain prophets and teachers ministered to the Lord and fasted, the Holy Ghost said, Separate me Barnabas and Saul for the work whereunto I have called them. . . . So they being sent forth by the Holy Ghost departed." Under his inspiration, Paul read the heart of Elymas. At An- tioch in Pisidia, notwithstanding bitter persecution, the disciples were filled with joy and with the Holy Ghost. He guided the deliberations of the Church in the first council at Jerusalem, for the apostles, and elders, and brethren wrote, " It seemed good to the Holy Ghost, and to us." He ordered the steps of Paul and Silas, forbidding them to preach the word in Proconsular Asia ; and when they assayed to go into Bithynia, suf- fering them not. Of the fulfilment of the promised effusion of the Holy Spirit, the disciples whom Paul found at Ephesus, had not heard; but their baptism with the Spirit laid the foundations of the Christian Church in that mighty city. Paul went up to Jeru- salem " bound in the Spirit," and hence was willing to endure the bonds, which the Holy Ghost by other messengers foretold awaited him there. He solemnly reminds the elders of Ephesus that the Holy Ghost had made them overseers of the Church, to feed the flock of God. And this was his final warning to the unbelieving Jews in Rome, ere he turned to the Gen- tiles, " Well spake the Holy Ghost by Esaias the

Acts x. 19, 38, 44—47; xi. 12, 15, 16: xv. 8.

ch. xi. 24, 28.

ch. xiii. 1—4.

ch. xiii. 9.

ch. xiii. 52.

ch. xv. 28.

ch. xvi. 6, 7

ch. xix. 6.

ch. xix. 21; xx. 22; xxi. 4, 11.

ch. xx. 28.

prophet, . . . Hearing ye shall hear, and shall not un- derstand." In this one book of Scripture, his sacred name occurs between fifty and sixty times.

Acts xxviii. 15.

In the Pauline epistles there are some chapters pecu- liarly rich in the glimpses they afford of the Holy Spirit's ministry, like constellations of pre-eminent brightness in the starry firmament. I may mention Rom. viii.; 1 Cor. ii. and xii.; 2 Cor. iii.; and Gal. v. But referring to the witness of these inspired letters in order, we are assured that every pulse of love which beats in our hearts Godwards is to be traced to the secret influence of the Holy Ghost.* Then the won- derful eighth chapter, I have named, speaks of believers as made free by the law of the Spirit of life; as walk- ing after the Spirit; as being after the Spirit, and minding the things of the Spirit; as being in the Spirit, who dwells in them, and is the unfailing test of discipleship, and who, being the Spirit of him that raised up Jesus from the dead, will be the Agent in

Rom. v. 5.

---

* The reader will observe that I have here passed over the expression "the Spirit of holiness," as below I pass over that "justified in the Spirit," and again that "quickened by the Spirit." I believe that in these three cases the reference is not to the third Person of the Holy Trinity, but to the human spirit of the incarnate Saviour as distinguished from his human flesh. Thus in Rom. i. 3, 4, Jesus Christ is said to be "made of the seed of David according to the flesh (κατὰ σάρκα), but de- clared to be the Son of God, with power according to the spirit of holiness" (κατὰ πνεῦμα ἁγιωσύνης)—spiritual holiness, abso- lute and indefectible, proving essential Deity, as in the heavenly song, "Thou only art holy." So in 1 Tim. iii. 18, "manifest in the flesh" (ἐν σαρκί), *i.e.*, in his human body, is distinguished from "justified in the spirit (ἐν πνεύματι), *i. e.*, in his human spirit, for not only in body but also in spirit was he proved the sinless and Holy One. And thus likewise in 1 Pet. iii. 18, having been put to death in [his human] flesh (σαρκί), but quickened in spirit (πνεύματι, omit τῷ with the best MSS.), our Lord's human body is contrasted with his disembodied human spirit.

ch. i. 4.
1 Tim. iii. 16.
1 Pet. iii. 18.

Rev. xv. 4.
John i. 14.

their resurrection; as through the Spirit mortifying the deeds of the body; as being led by the Spirit, who is in them the Spirit of adoption, and bears witness with their spirit that they are the children of God; and as now possessing only the firstfruits of the Spirit who helps their infirmities in prayer, and so makes intercession in them and for them that he who searches the heart recognises in their desires the minding of the Spirit. There are seventeen references in that chapter to his work; and afterwards in the same epistle St. Paul appeals to Him as attesting his love for Israel, names "joy in the Holy Ghost," as the highest characteristic of the kingdom of God, pleads that those to whom he wrote might abound in hope through the power of the Holy Ghost, trusts that the offering up of the Gentiles will be acceptable "being sanctified by the Holy Ghost," and affirms that in his might alone were the miracles, he wrought, accomplished, and finally entreats their prayers on his behalf, urging this most touching plea, "For the Lord Jesus Christ's sake and for the love of the Spirit." Rom. ix. 1. ch. xiv. 17. ch. xv. 13, 16, 19, 30.

In the second chapter of the first epistle to the Corinthians, St. Paul not only says that his preaching was "in demonstration of the Spirit and of power," but declares plainly that God had by his Spirit revealed to them (*i. e.* to himself and the other inspired apostles and through their teaching to all faithful students of the word) mysteries which eye hath not seen nor ear heard; that the Spirit searcheth all things, even the depths of God, and knows the things of God, even as the spirit of man knows the things of a man; and that they had received this Spirit, which is of God, by whose teaching they spoke God-taught words, unintelligible to the natural man, but understood and embraced by all who were born of the Spirit. Twice

after this he affirms that the bodies of saints are the
temples of the Holy Ghost. This Spirit seals their
justification. This Spirit authorizes the apostle's legis-
lation for the Church. And then in the twelfth chapter
he unfolds the marvellous and manifold operations of
the Spirit in the Church, to whom every faithful confession of Christ as the Lord is alone due, whose diversities of gifts, whether manifested as the word of
wisdom, or as the word of knowledge, or as faith, or as
the gifts of healing, or as the working of miracles, or
as prophecy, or as discerning of spirits, or as divers
kinds of tongues, or as the interpretation of tongues,
are wrought by that one and the selfsame Spirit who
divides to every man severally as he wills. This is
that Spirit by whom we are all baptized into one body
and into whom we have all been made to drink.

In the second letter to that Church we read of "the
earnest of the Spirit in our hearts." And we are
solemnly reminded that all saints are epistles of
Christ written with the Spirit of the living God; that
the ministers of the new covenant are employed by the
Spirit who alone makes the word quick and powerful;
that the gospel is the ministration of the Spirit; that
where the Spirit of the Lord is, there is liberty; and
that it is our holy privilege to worship with unveiled
face, and thus to be changed into the same image from
glory to glory as by the Lord the Spirit. By the
Holy Ghost was the apostle's ministry approved. This
was his zealous fear for the children in the faith lest
they should receive another spirit than that which they
had received already. And this was his closing benediction: "The grace of the Lord Jesus Christ, and
the love of God, and the communion of the Holy Ghost
be with you all."

In like godly jealousy he warns the Galatians, lest

1 Cor. iii. 16;
vi. 19.

ch. vi. 11.

ch. vii. 40.

ch. xii. 3—13.

2 Cor. i. 22.

ch. iii. 3, 6, 8,
17, 18.

ch. vi. 6.

ch. xi. 4.

ch. xiii. 14.

having " received the Spirit by the hearing of faith,"
and having thus " begun in the Spirit," they should
seek to be made perfect by the flesh; he reminds them
that God ministered to them the Spirit and so wrought
miracles among them; and thus he leads them on to
the glorious design of Christ's eternal redemption, viz.,
" that we might receive the promise of the Spirit
through faith." This is that Spirit of his Son, whom
God sends into our hearts, crying Abba, Father.
Through this Spirit we wait for the hope of righteousness; in him we walk and war a good warfare: by
him we are led: and he it is who produces in us his
own heavenly fruits—love, joy, peace, long-suffering,
gentleness, goodness, faith, meekness, temperance; thus
must we live, thus walk in the Spirit. And thus
sowing to the Spirit here we shall of the Spirit reap
life everlasting.

The epistle to the Ephesians is scarcely less rich in
its allusions to the work of the Divine Spirit, that
Holy Spirit of promise whereby believers are sealed,
and whom the Father of glory vouchsafes as the Spirit
of wisdom and revelation: that One Spirit by whom
Jews and Gentiles have access through Jesus Christ
unto the Father, and in whom they are builded together for an habitation of God; that Spirit who revealed
the mystery of Christ to the holy apostles and prophets
of the New Covenant, and by whom every member of
the whole family is strengthened with might in the
inner man; that One Spirit, who is the alone Author
of true unity, who in gracious fellowship with the
human spirit renews our mind, and whose tender love
we are so urgently entreated not to grieve; that Spirit
whose fruit is in all goodness, and righteousness, and
truth, the fullest measure of whose indwelling grace
we are charged to strive after; and lastly, whose sword

Marginal references:
Gal. iii. 2, 3, 5, 14.
ch. iv. 6.
ch. v. 5, 16, 17, 18, 22 —25.
ch. vi. 8.
Eph. i. 13, 17
ch. ii. 18, 22.
ch. iii. 5, 16.
ch. iv. 3, 4, 23, 30.
ch. v. 9, 18.

the word of God is declared to be, and in whom alone
suppliants can pray with persevering and successful
Eph. vi. 17, 18. prayer.

In the epistle to the Philippians we learn that all
the apostle's hope rested on " the supply of the Spirit
of Jesus Christ;" that he numbers " the fellowship of
the Spirit" among the strongest of all pleas which he
could urge; and that he counts this as an essential
mark of all who are Christ's, " they worship God in
Spirit;" or, following many of the best MSS. " they
Phil. i. 19; ii. 1; iii. 3. worship the Spirit of God."*   In that to the Colossians
we see that all the love which characterized the glow-
Col. i. 8. ing Church at Colosse subsisted " in the Spirit."
And in those to the Thessalonians we are reminded
that " the gospel came to them not in word only, but
in power and in the Holy Ghost," and was received by
them with his heavenly joy though in much affliction;
that they were warned against impurity, lest haply
they should despise the Giver of the Holy Spirit; whose
sacred fire they must not quench as they valued the

---

* The received text is οἱ πνεύματι Θεῷ λατρεύοντες, which
would admit of the translation given in our authorized version,
though not necessitating it, as this might be rendered "who
worship the Spirit as God."   But the reading Θεοῦ rests upon
the authority of almost all the best MSS., including the
Sinaitic, and is adopted by Wordsworth, Alford, Ellicott, and all
modern editors.   It is true that many who adopt this reading
would render the clause, "who by the Spirit of God are serving,"
taking λατρεύοντες absolutely; but this seems very harsh when
one who is the object of adoration is named immediately before.
And the judgment of the sagacious Poole seems here to be preferred, who says, " Alii legunt Θεοῦ, ita vertendum, *qui Spiritui
Dei servimus.   Hinc colligitur Spiritum Sanctum esse Deum, cui
cultus debetur.*"   "Others read Θεοῦ, and we must then translate
the clause, *Who serve the Spirit of God.*   And from this we may
Poli Synopsis. prove that the Holy Spirit is God, to whom adoration is due."
So the Coptic version renders it, *Who worship the Spirit of God.*

CHAP. I.

life of God within them: and when that marvellous chain of salvation is revealed, stretching from eternal election unto eternal glory, these middle links hold their necessary place, " through sanctification of the Spirit and belief of the truth." 1 Thess. i. 5, 6; iv. 8; v. 19.

The Pastoral epistles contain the express prophecy of the Spirit regarding the great apostasy from the faith; certify believers that the Spirit which God hath given them is the Spirit of power, and of love, and of a sound mind; warn ministers to keep that which has been committed to them, by the Holy Ghost, and bear witness to that Divine mercy wherewith God hath saved us by the washing of regeneration and renewal of the Holy Ghost. 2 Thess. ii. 13, 14. 1 Tim. iv. 1 —3. 2 Tim. i. 7, 14. Tit. iii. 5.

The epistle to the Hebrews testifies that the signs and wonders and divers miracles wrought by the heralds of the gospel were accompanied with " gifts," or " distributions," of the Holy Ghost; and that those who were once enlightened and tasted of the heavenly gift were made partakers of that same Spirit. Here also a quotation from the Psalms bears the solemn imprimatur: " The Holy Ghost saith." Here the typical import of the tabernacle is ascribed to him, " The Holy Ghost this signifying." And here the sacrifice of the Lamb of God is said to have been offered through the Eternal Spirit. Heb. ii. 4; vi. 4. ch. iii. 7; see also ch. x. 15. ch. ix. 8. ch. ix. 14.

St. James solemnly asks, " Doth the Spirit which abode in you yearn toward envy?"* St. Peter, in his ch. iv. 5.

---

* James iv. 5. *Think ye that the Scripture speaketh in vain?* The apostle probably refers to such urgent intreaties and such awful warnings as Deut. x. 12—20; xxviii. 15—68. Are these mere idle words? *Doth the Spirit which abode in you*—that Good Spirit wherewith ye were sealed—*yearn toward envy?* Nay, verily, but towards love. The interpretations of this verse are almost endless; but the above, which is adopted by Calvin,

first epistle, affirms that saints are " elect unto obedience through sanctification of the Spirit;" that it was the Spirit of Christ in the Old Testament prophets who fore-announced the sufferings and glory of Messiah; that the preachers of the gospel proclaimed the glad tidings " with the Holy Ghost sent down from heaven," that they who received that gospel " purified their souls in obeying the truth through the Spirit;" and that on those who were reproached for the name of 1 Pet. 1, 2, 11, Christ, the Spirit of glory and of God rested : and in his second epistle he bears this emphatic testimony to the inspiration of the oracles of God, " Prophecy came not of old time by the will of man; but holy men of God spake as they were moved by the Holy Ghost." St. John in his first epistle, not only dwells on the unction from the Holy One which abides in all saints, but gives this test of true discipleship, " Hereby we know that he abideth in us by his Spirit which he hath given us;" declares that the Spirit of God, who is the Spirit of truth, ever confesses the incarnation of the Word ; and affirms that the Spirit is One of Three who bears witness because the Spirit is truth.   And St. Jude, while characterizing the ungodly, as " having not the Spirit," charges us—" Building up yourselves in your most holy faith, praying in the Holy Ghost, keep yourselves in the love of God, looking for the mercy of our Lord Jesus Christ unto eternal life."

And when we come to that mysterious and glorious book which closes the canon of the New Testament, the opening benediction is from the sevenfold Spirit in union with the Eternal Father and the Eternal Son : the apostle saw all the visions, which he records, in the

1 Pet. 1, 2, 11,
12, 22, and
iv. 14.

2 Pet. i. 21.

1 John ii. 20,
27.

ch. iii. 24;
see also
ch. iv. 13.

ch. v. 6—8.

Jude 19, 20.

Rev. i. 4; see
also ch. iii.
1; iv. 5;
v. 6.

Scholefield, Wordsworth, etc., obviates all the difficulty which those encounter who view the second clause as a quotation from Scripture.

Spirit: the messages to the seven churches were all the words of the Spirit: the witnesses are raised by the Spirit of life from God: the Spirit testifies to the blessedness of those who die in the Lord: the testimony of Jesus is declared to be the Spirit of prophecy: and the latest sweetest invitation of evangel love is proclaimed by the Spirit and the Bride.

Rev. i. 10; iv. 2; xvii. 3; xxi. 10.
ch. ii. 7, 11, 17, 29; iii. 6, 13, 22.
ch. xi. 11.
ch. xiv. 13.
ch. xix. 10.

ch. xxii. 17.

And here the question recurs which was suggested after the review of the Old Testament Scriptures, namely, whether we are able to trace in the New Testament likewise any progressive development and revelation of the work of the Holy Spirit? I venture to think such a gradual unfolding is discernible. In the three synoptic gospels, Matthew, Mark, and Luke, the light which reveals his gracious dispensation grows stronger and stronger from the first intimations to the Virgin and Joseph and Zacharias and Simeon to the preaching of John, and the visible descent of the Holy Spirit upon our Lord at his baptism, anointing him for his ministry and death and resurrection. In the Acts we have the work of the Spirit in the Church, from the day of Pentecost at Jerusalem, in ever widening circles of blessing, until the gospel standard is planted within the walls of Rome: herein is seen the ecclesiastical governance and jurisdiction of the Spirit, resting as tongues of fire on the disciples, opening the door of life to the Gentiles, appointing overseers of the flock, guiding their counsels, and warning them of the eternal issues involved in the acceptance or rejection of the gospel. If, however, in the Acts we can take a wide survey, as with a field telescope, of the Holy Spirit's administration and of the Church's warfare, in the Epistles of St. Paul and St. Peter we are permitted to inspect, as with a powerful microscope, his Divine operations in the heart of the believer, as the soul is transformeᴅ from glory to glory into the image of Jesus Christ: the Acts bring before us especially his *objective* work, and the Epistles his *subjective* creation. But it was reserved for John the Beloved, who wrote at the close of the first century, in his gospel, and letters, and Apocalypse, to set forth in all its fulness the mystery of the mission of the Comforter, the unction from the Holy One which abides in all his children, and the unveiling by his prescient grace of the Church's conflicts and everlasting victory in the glories of the New Jerusalem.

But at least on a review of the whole evidence of Scripture we may fearlessly assert that from Genesis to Revelation there is an unbroken chain of testimony to the abiding presence in the Church militant of this Great Spirit, most awful in his majesty, most gentle in his meekness, and most mysterious in his working. And the question must present itself to every patient prayerful student, Who is this wonderful Being? Who is he, that I may know him, and, if he be God, may adore, and trust, and love him with every affection of my soul?

CHAPTER II

THE PERSONALITY OF THE HOLY GHOST

THE Scriptures adduced in the previous chapter prove CHAP. II.
the continual presence and operation in heaven and
earth of a mighty mysterious Being, called, the Spirit,
the Spirit of God, the Spirit of Jehovah, the Spirit
of your Father, the Spirit of his Son, or, his most
frequent designation, the Holy Spirit or Ghost.* That
this Being is not to be confounded with the Father
and the Son appears from all those passages in Holy
Writ, which reveal to us the simultaneous co-operation
or manifestation of three infinite Agents.

Thus when we read, " From the time that it was,
there am I: and now the Lord God and his Spirit hath
sent me," if the Spirit is not here to be distinguished Isa. xlviii. 16.
from the Lord God, wherefore is he declared to be

---

* The words *Spirit* and *Ghost* are used interchangeably in
the Authorized Version. *Spirit* (Latin *spiritus* from *spiro* to
breathe, possibly derived from σπαίρω or ἀσπαίρω to pant)
simply signifies *breath* or *air in motion*. *Ghost* appears in Saxon
as *gast*, in German as *geist*, in Danish as *geest*, in Irish as
gasda, and seems to be derived radically from some word signifying to *move* or *rush*; Irish, *gaisim* to flow ; English, *gush, gust*
(see Webster under " Ghost" and " Ghastly "). So that the
Hebrew רוּחַ (spirit or breath or wind), the Greek πνεῦμα
(from πνέω, to breathe), the Latin *spiritus*, and the old English
ghost, all suggest the breathing or moving of air, and are all
nearly equivalent.

associated with him in this mission of Messiah ? or if not to be distinguished from Messiah, then the Sender and the Sent are one and the same person, which is impossible. Again, it is written, " The Spirit of the Lord God is upon me, because Jehovah hath anointed me," and who can here confuse the unction of the Spirit with the Lord God who anoints, or with the Ambassador who is anointed ? And once more it is foretold, " I will pour upon the house of David and upon the inhabitants of Jerusalem the Spirit of grace and of supplication, and they shall look upon me whom they have pierced and mourn for him ;" is this Spirit of grace to be identified with the one who pours forth that Spirit or with the pierced Saviour, for whom he teaches Israel to mourn ?

But let us come to the New Testament. We open the gospel history and read, " Now when all the people were baptized, it came to pass that Jesus also being baptized, and praying, the heaven was opened, and the Holy Ghost descended in a bodily shape like a dove upon him, and a voice came from heaven which said, Thou art my beloved Son ; in thee I am well pleased ;" and we are compelled to say that the descending Spirit is distinct from the praying Saviour and from the approving Father. We listen to the gracious promise, " I will pray the Father, and he shall give you another Comforter that he may abide with you for ever, even the Spirit of truth ;" and as we distinguish between the Son who intercedes and the Father who gives, so do we distinguish that other Comforter from both. We find in the great evangelistic charge these words, " baptizing them in the name of the Father, and of the Son, and of the Holy Ghost ," and we cannot obliterate the personal distinction here affirmed. We ponder the marvellous scene

Isa. lxi. 1.

Zech. xii. 10.

Luke iii. 21, 22.

John xiv. 16, 17.

Matt. xxviii. 19.

of the first Pentecost of the Christian Church, and hear
the apostle Peter saying, " This Jesus hath God raised
up whereof we all are witnesses : therefore being by
the right hand of God exalted, and having received of
the Father the promise of the Holy Ghost, he hath
shed forth this which ye now see and hear ;" and we Acts ii. 32, 33
can neither identify that Spirit, who sat in the likeness
of cloven tongues of fire on the disciples, with the risen
Jesus, nor with the Father at whose right hand Jesus
was exalted.   The same impossibility of refusing to
recognise a distinction plainly intended and affirmed
would attach to many passages in the epistles, such as
Rom. viii. 16, 17 ; 1 Cor. xii. 4—6 ; 2 Cor. xiii. 14 ;
Gal. iv. 4—6 ; Eph. ii. 18 : iv. 4—6 ; 2 Thess. ii.
13, 14 ; Tit. iii. 4—6 ; Heb. x. 29, 30 ; 1 Pet. i. 2 ;
Jude 20, 21.   And when in the Apocalypse, the benediction of grace and peace is besought " from (ἀπό),
Him which is and which was and which is to come,
and from (καὶ ἀπό) the seven spirits which are before
his throne, and from (καὶ ἀπό) Jesus Christ, the
faithful witness," we can only conclude that there is a Rev. i. 4, 5.
source of spiritual strength for the Church of God,
a source which is threefold and yet one, one and yet
threefold.

In this stage of our enquiry it will be enough to ask
ourselves, In the cases cited above, was the co-operating
Spirit identical with the Father or with the Son?
Could you for example say that the apparent Spirit
who descended on our Lord at his baptism, or whose
fiery symbol sat upon the disciples on the day of Pentecost, was the Father or the Son?   No one could
maintain this for a moment.   And the difficulty,
though more removed from observation, in the other
Scriptures referred to, would be equally real and insu-
perable.   We are therefore compelled to acknowledge

that the Holy Ghost cannot be identified or confounded with the Eternal Father or with his Son Jesus Christ our Lord.

But further not only is the Spirit of God to be distinguished from the Father and the Son, which might be affirmed of the love of God or the grace of Christ, but such personal properties, and capacities, and actions are ascribed in Holy Scripture to this Spirit, as prove independent and intelligent personality.

It is freely admitted that there are several Scriptures in which the term *Spirit* or *Spirit of God* is used to signify the gifts and graces of the Spirit, as when we read of the Spirit being poured out upon the Church; or of a double portion of the Spirit being given to Elisha; or of the Spirit, which was upon Moses, being taken by God and put upon the seventy elders. Here an objector asks, If the Spirit were a person, how could he be thus effused or divided? But to this it is quite sufficient to answer, that in such cases by a very frequent figure of speech the influences and effects are described by the source from which they flow. The question is not whether some passages may not be brought forward which denote the operations and influences of the Spirit, and therefore do *not* establish his personality, but besides these, whether there are not very numerous passages of Holy Writ which *do* positively assert and prove it. Just as if I were studying a work of horticulture, and because the writer here and there used the term " sun " to denote the radiance of the sun, directing me to place certain plants *in the sun*, or that *more or less sun* should be admitted, I were to contend that the author could not believe there was actually such a globe of light in the heavens, although in many other parts of his book he had spoken in strictly astronomical language of our planetary system.

You would justly answer me that the occasional occurrence of such familiar phrases as " more or less sun," etc. was no valid argument against his conviction of the sun's real existence stated elsewhere in the volume plainly and positively. So we admit that by the Spirit are sometimes intended the gifts and graces of the Spirit. These graces may be poured out, these gifts distributed. These diverse manifestations of the Spirit are given to every man to profit withal. But, the apostle adds, "All these worketh that one and the self-same Spirit, dividing to every man severally as he wills." 1 Cor. xii. 11.

It is of that ONE SPIRIT we write. Now according to the Scriptures (1) He possesses such qualities as a person only can possess: (2) He performs such actions as a person only can perform: (3) He is capable of suffering such injuries as a person only can suffer : and (4) He is expressly called another Comforter, and is designated by the use of masculine pronouns, though the noun itself, Spirit, is neuter.

(1) He possesses such qualities as a person only can possess. What are the chief qualities of a person ? Are they not intelligence, affection, will ? Now the Scripture testifies of—

The knowledge of the Spirit. " God hath revealed them to us by his Spirit ; for the Spirit searcheth all things, yea, the depths ($\tau\grave{a}$ $\beta\acute{a}\theta\eta$) of God : for what man knoweth the things of a man save the spirit of man which is in him ? even so the things of God knoweth no man but the Spirit of God." That the ch. ii. 10, 11. Spirit here is not a mere quality of Divine nature, as consciousness is of the human mind, appears from the first clause, " God hath revealed them to us by his Spirit," which clearly implies a personal distinction, for it could not be said that a man makes anything known to others by his consciousness." Pye Smith.

The Divine love of the Spirit. " I beseech you," writes St. Paul, "for the love of the Spirit" (διὰ τῆς ἀγάπης τοῦ Πνεύματος): a plea exactly corresponding with one he had used shortly before. " I beseech you by the mercies of God" (διὰ τῶν οἰκτιρμῶν τοῦ Θεοῦ) : — and a personal quality, which could alone enable him to perform his gracious office of " shedding abroad the love of God in the hearts" of believers.

Rom. xv. 30;
xii. 1 ; and
v. 5.

And *The self-determining will of the Spirit.* Thus, as quoted above, he divides his gifts to every man severally as he wills (καθὼς βούλεται). Compare also John iii. 8; Acts xvi. 6, 7. Now will is the very essence of personality. Perhaps there is no stronger argument against the tenets of Sabellius, who would have confounded the personality of the Father and the Son, than the words of our Lord, " I came down from heaven not to do mine own will but the will of him that sent me." The same proof, seeing that the Spirit likewise possesses a self-regulating will, establishes his personality.

John vi. 38.

(2) The Spirit performs such actions as a person only can perform. Thus we read in Scripture,

He created the worlds and gives life to those who live.

Psa. xxxiii.
6; Job
xxxiii. 4;
Isa. xl. 13.
Gen. vi. 3.
John xvi. 8.
Ezek. iii. 12;
viii. 3;
Acts ii. 4;
viii. 39;
Rom. xv.
19.
Luke i. 35.
2 Pet. i. 21.
1 Tim. iv. 1.

Rev. ii. 7, etc.

Acts xx. 28.

He strives with the ungodly.

He convicts the world of sin, righteousness, and judgment.

He performs miracles.

He caused the Virgin Mary to conceive.

He inspired the sacred writers.

He speaks expressly of events in the latter times.

He saith to the Churches the messages of the Son of Man.

He appoints ministers in the Church.

He commands and forbids.

He new creates the soul.

He intercedes for us in prayer.

He teaches, and comforts, and guides us into all truth.

He sheds abroad the love of God in the heart.

He seals the soul unto the day of redemption.

He cries in our heart, until he teaches us to cry, *Abba, Father.*

He testifies with personal witnesses. " He shall testify (μαρτυρήσει) and ye also testify (μαρτυρεῖτε)."

He approves with personal counsellors. " It seemed good to the Holy Ghost and to us."

He invites with personal messengers. " The Spirit and the Bride say, Come."

He repeats the beatitude pronounced on those who die in the Lord. " Yea, saith the Spirit, they rest from their labours and their works do follow them."

Here are some twenty different actions, some of them standing forth as the greatest facts in the past history of the Church of Christ, and many of them being repeated continually in the experience of believers, but all proving beyond contradiction, the operation of an Intelligent and Personal Agent.

(3) The Spirit is capable of suffering such injuries as a person only can suffer.

He can be vexed. For we read of Israel. " They returned and vexed,* (וְעִצְּבוּ, which the LXX render

Marginal references:
- Acts viii. 29; xi. 12; xiii. 2; xvi. 6, 7. John iii. 5—8; Tit. iii. 5.
- Rom. viii. 26.
- John xiv. 26.
- Rom. v. 5.
- Ephes. iv. 30.
- Compare Gal iv. 6, with Rom. viii 15.
- John xv. 26, 27.
- Acts xv. 28.
- Rev. xxii. 17
- ch. xiv. 13.

---

* The word עָצַב is translated " grieved," Gen. vi. 6; xxxiv. 7; xlv. 5; 1 Sam. xx. 3, 34; 2 Sam. xix. 2; 1 Chron. iv. 10; Nehem. viii. 11; Psa. lxxviii. 40; Isa. liv. 6: " displeased," 1 Kings i. 6; " be sorry," Neh. viii. 10, and in all these cases implies the anguish of a sorrowing heart. The only other in-

παρώξυναν) his Holy Spirit, " therefore he was turned to be their enemy."

He can be grieved.   For we are entreated, " Grieve not (μὴ λυπεῖτε) the Holy Spirit of God."

He can be blasphemed.   For we are solemnly warned, " He that shall blaspheme against (βλασφημήσῃ εἰς) the Holy Ghost hath never forgiveness."

He can be lied against and tempted.   For St. Peter demanded of Ananias, " Why hath Satan filled thine heart to lie to (ψεύσασθαι, to attempt to deceive) the Holy Ghost?" and of Sapphira his wife, " How is it that ye have agreed together to tempt (πειράσαι) the Spirit of the Lord?"

He can be insulted.   For in the Epistle to the Hebrews we read that the wilful and persevering apostate " hath done despite to (ἐνυβρίσας) the Spirit of grace."   I do not here bring forward the awful charge of St. Stephen against the Jews, " Ye do always resist (ἀντιπίπτετε, dash as waves against a rock) the Holy Ghost; as your fathers did, so do ye," for such resistance is conceivable against impersonal power or influence. But with regard to the other Scriptures adduced, would it be possible to speak of an influence being vexed grieved, blasphemed, lied against, tempted, insulted ?

(4) *The Spirit is expressly called another Comforter, and is designated by the use of masculine pronouns, though the noun itself, Spirit, is neuter.*

Thus in the memorable promise, " I will pray the Father and he shall give you another Comforter," (ἄλλον Παράκλητον) the very name Comforter implies a personal advocate, helper, consoler.*   None but an

Isa. lxiii. 10.

Ephes. iv. 30.

Mark iii. 29.

Acts v. 3, 9.

Heb. x. 29.

Acts vii. 51.

John xiv. 16.

---

stances of its occurrence in the Old Testament are Job x. 8 ; Psa. lvi. 5 ; Eccl. x. 9 ; Jer. xliv. 19.

* The word *Paraclete*, as used in the New Testament, represents two Hebrew words, (1) מְנַחֵם (*menachem*), " a Com-

intelligent, loving person, who could discriminate and
sympathize, and minister timely aid, could fulfil the
office of a Comforter. Such Jesus Christ promises the
Spirit of truth shall be. Such he was himself; and as
such bears the same name, " We have an advocate
(Παράκλητον) with the Father, Jesus Christ the
righteous." And moreover he here distinguishes BE-
TWIXT himself and the one whom the Father would
send in his name by designating him as ANOTHER Comforter. So Augustine, quoted by Wordsworth, says,
" By calling the person here promised to be sent,
another Paraclete" he shows that there is one
person, who sends, of the Son; and another to be sent,

1 John ii. 1

---

forter," for which the LXX had used παρακλήτωρ in Job xvi. 2 :
one of the names of Messiah was *Menahem*, " the Consolation of
Israel," And (2) מֵלִיץ (*melits*), an interpreter or mediator,
an advocate called in to plead a cause, or a friendly assistant
in a judicial suit, for which the Chaldee paraphrasts use פרקלים
(*praclit*), *i. e.*, παράκλητος. Hence paraclete sometimes signifies
one who consoles and comforts by counsel and aid, and sometimes
one who mediates or interprets, and presents petitions to another
as an intercessor."—Wordsworth. Archdeacon Hare says, " If
we understand the word *comforter* not merely in its secondary
and common sense as consoler, but also in its primary and
etymological sense as strengthener and supporter, it would be
difficult to find any word in our language so well fitted to express
a range of meaning corresponding to that embraced by the Greek
(παράκλητος), although etymologically different. For though
confortare [conforto, *i. e.*, " fortem facio," *I strengthen*, " con-
solor," *I comfort*, Facciolati] is scarcely found in classical Latin,
it is common in the Vulgate. It is continually used by Wiclif
to represent its Latin original, *e. g.*, in Luke xxii. 43, *And an
aungel apperide to him fro hevene, and confortide him* (con-
fortans eum). Let us only practically remember that the comfort
of the Holy Ghost is what the apostle emphatically calls *strong consolation* (ἰσχυρὰν παράκλησιν). Such was Christ's consolation,
when he said to the widow of Nain " Weep not;" and immediately
added the word of power, " Young man, I say unto thee, Arise."

See Luke ii. 25

See JOD xxxiii. 23

Acts ix. 19; Phil. iv. 13, etc., " Mission of the Comforter," Note, Ja., pp. 523, 524. Heb. vi. 18.

of the Holy Ghost." And Chrysostom, " By the word *another* Christ shows the distinction of persons; by the word *Paraclete* he declares the equality of dignity."*

But further, although the noun itself ($\pi\nu\epsilon\hat{\upsilon}\mu a$), *Spirit*, is neuter, the Comforter here promised is designated by the use of masculine pronouns.

" But the Comforter, the Holy Ghost, which (ὸ) the Father will send in my name, he ($\dot{\epsilon}\kappa\epsilon\hat{\imath}\nu o\varsigma$, that John xiv. 26. Person) shall teach you all things."

But when the Comforter is come, whom (ὸν) I will send unto you from the Father, even the Spirit of truth which (ὸ) proceedeth from the Father, he ($\dot{\epsilon}\kappa\epsilon\hat{\imath}\nu o\varsigma$) ch. xv. 26. shall testify of me."

" Howbeit, when he, the Spirit of truth ($\dot{\epsilon}\kappa\epsilon\hat{\imath}\nu o\varsigma$ τὸ Πνεῦμα ἀληθείας) is come, etc.: he ($\dot{\epsilon}\kappa\epsilon\hat{\imath}\nu o\varsigma$) shall ch. xvi. 13, glorify me," etc.
14.

Apart from the actions ascribed to him, the very phraseology here employed by our Lord, which is equivalent to " That Spiritual Essence Himself (not itself)," strongly evidences the personal nature of the Holy Ghost. And in strict accordance with this St. Paul writes, " Ye were sealed with the Holy Spirit of Eph. i. 13, 14. promise, who (ὸς)† is the earnest of our inheritance."

Surely from a calm and comprehensive study of this testimony gathered from the word of God, we must conclude that if these qualities, and actions, and capacities, and designations, do not prove personality, there are none, however explicit and exact, which can do so. Unitarians are wont to speak of the Spirit, as an effusion or emanation separate from God, or as an influence or power exercised by God. Can you speak of the

---

* On this Bengel tersely writes, "Alius paracletus ipse ab alio distinctus est; et alterius officium ab alterius officio differt."

† It is to be regretted that the force of this is lost in the indiscriminate " which " of our translation.

intelligence, or of the love, or of the will of an effusion ? Can you speak of an emanation, or influence or aught impersonal creating and quickening that which it creates ; striving with the obstinate and convicting them of their error; performing miracles; addressing others in express words; appointing officers; commanding and forbidding; renewing that which was lapsed; interceding, teaching, comforting, and guiding into truth; diffusing love and filial tenderness in the heart; witnessing with those who witness; approving with those who approve, and inviting with those who invite; and revealing the blessedness of those unseen? Can you speak of a mere abstract power being vexed, grieved, blasphemed, lied against, tempted, insulted ? Can you speak of an impersonal essence as Himself? If in some few instances you might thus personify an influence, most of those adduced taken singly resist such an interpretation ; and, taken collectively, would, if thus understood, confuse all the laws of language and thus derange the first principles of truth.

Conventional phrases too easily obscure our view. Let me venture an hypothesis. Suppose that from St. Paul's use of the word " power " in the epistle to the Romans, " There is no power (ἐξουσία) but of God: . . whosoever therefore resisteth the power, re-sisteth the ordinance of God: . . wilt thou then not be afraid of the power? Do that which is good, and thou shalt have praise of the same, for he is a minister of God to thee for good," had arisen the custom of naming the viceroy of a king, his majesty's power. And suppose that in the volume of history you met with the following passage :—" The prince having left this in-surgent province, thought good that his majesty's power should occupy his room: as for this power, he knew the most secret counsels of the king; his will

Rom. xiii. 1—4.

and actions were independent; he strove with the ill-affected, and was grieved and vexed with the obstinacy of some, while others he convinced of their infatuation and was enabled to train as good citizens; he consoled the well-disposed; he issued commands and restrictions at his own pleasure; he appointed and deposed subordinate officers; he spoke expressly of the certain issue of some incipient plots; he accomplished prodigies of benevolence: indeed, such was the authority of this power that whoever wilfully insulted him was by the king's command reserved for judgment; while on the other hand his majesty's power was accustomed to repeat assurances which came direct from court of the favour awarded there to faithful subjects." Could you doubt for a moment whether or not this power was a personal intelligent agent? And if, a few pages further on, you read, " And thus his majesty's power was extended and his dominion consolidated," would you, because of the introduction or repetition of the term *power* or *his majesty's power*, confuse the latter abstraction with the former person? It is impossible. You would say, Honest language, though capable of metaphor, is incapable of such delusive impersonations. So likewise Scripture from the very beginning had established the usage of naming that mysterious Being, whose nature we are humbly studying, as *the Spirit*, or *the Spirit of God*, or *the Spirit of Jehovah*. It is true there are passages of Holy Writ in which the term describes his graces or gifts. But looking at the whole inspired word, its testimony is unambiguous and irresistible that the Divine Spirit is a living Agent working with intelligent consciousness, and independent will, and infinite love.

But how solemn is this conclusion. In dealing with the Holy Spirit (and he strives to enter or dwells in every heart) we have to do, not with an impersonal influence however vast, but with a personal Be'ng whose quick sensibilities can be grieved, whose vigilant love can be gratified, whose forbearance may be exhausted by those who resist him, but whose sympathy with those who yield to his voice is more tender than that of the tenderest parent, or brother, or friend.

CHAPTER III

THE ETERNAL GODHEAD OF THE HOLY SPIRIT

THE personality of the Holy Ghost has been proved to rest on the firmest and widest basis of Scripture testimony. It remains for us to consider the proof of his essential Deity. This is a distinct subject of inquiry. For example, it were easy to prove the personality of David or St. John from the individual character of each, from the works they wrought, and the sufferings they endured. But these characteristics, and actions, and passions were those of men, not of God; human, not Divine; such as appertain to the creature, and not to the Creator. With regard to the Holy Ghost, however, such are the attributes which he is represented as possessing, such the operations which he performs, such the supreme dignity which Scripture, by comparing spiritual things with spiritual, ascribes to him, and such the intimate relationship in which he stands to the Father and the Son, that One to whom these qualities are attributed, and by whom these actions are wrought, and with whom the Father and the Son are thus associated in glory and worship, must needs be none other than God over all, blessed for ever. Let us pursue these four independent, but converging lines of proof.

1. The Holy Spirit's attributes are those of Godhead.

He is Omnipresent. For this I first appeal to the direct testimony of the Psalmist. " Whither shall I go from thy Spirit? or whither shall I flee from thy presence? If I ascend up into heaven, thou art there : if I make my bed in hell, behold thou art there." Psa. cxxxix. 7, 8. Having already proved the personality of the Spirit, this Scripture affirms his omnipresence, for it declares it to be impossible to find any spot, however remote, in the boundless universe from which he is absent. And the same truth appears from the gracious work he is carrying on in ten thousand thousand hearts, not on earth only, but also in heaven, at one and the same time. When the Lord Jesus says, " Where two or three are gathered together in my name, there am I in the midst of them," we argue from it, and rightly, his Matt. xviii. 20. omnipresent Deity. The argument regarding the Holy Spirit is the same. " Whither shall I go from thy Spirit ?" is the language of every saint in every clime, of the assemblies of God's people through the length and breadth of Christendom, of those scattered far off among the heathen, of the blessed dead who rest from their labours, of the angels before the throne. Each and all adore the presence of the same Spirit. Go where you will, he is there. He fills heaven and earth.*

He is Omniscient. Not only, as before proved, is the Holy Spirit a personal Being possessed of intelligent understanding ; but his knowledge embraces infinity and spans eternity. Jesus says, " No one (οὐδείς) knoweth the Son but the Father, neither knoweth any one (τις) the Father save the Son." ch. xi. 27.

---

* See a noble passage in the treatise of Didymus *De Spiritu Sancto,* cap. 6, in which he proves the increate and uncircumscribed nature of the Holy Spirit from his dwelling in and sanctifying all saints and angels at one and the same time.

___

But of the Divine Spirit. we read, "The Spirit searcheth * all things, yea, the depths of God; for what man knoweth the things of a man save the spirit of man which is in him? even so the things of God knoweth no one ($o\dot{v}\delta\epsilon\iota\varsigma$) but the Spirit of God." Thus he alone, with the infinite Son, comprehends the incomprehensible Jehovah. The most intimate counsels, yea, the essential depths of Deity are open to his scrutiny. By his knowledge as embracing the past he has revealed in the Scriptures, which are written by his inspiration, things which took place before men drew breath, and even before the foundations of the world were laid; and by his prescience of the future he discloses "things to come." Thus he answers Jehovah's challenge, "Where wast thou, when I laid the foundations of the earth? declare, if thou hast understanding," etc.; and thinks it not robbery to share the glory of him who says, "Remember the former things of old; for I am God, and there is none else; I am God and there is none like me, declaring the end from the beginning and from ancient times the things which are not yet done, saying, My counsel shall stand, and I will do all my pleasure." Yesterday, to-day, and for ever are bared to his view.

He is Eternal. Here it would be enough to quote the apostle's words, "How much more shall the blood of Christ who through the Eternal Spirit ($\delta\iota\grave{a}$ $\Pi\nu\epsilon\acute{v}\mu\alpha\tau\circ\varsigma$ $\alpha\grave{\iota}\omega\nu\acute{\iota}ov$)† offered himself without spot to God purge your conscience," etc. This is the same word which is used of the everlasting God ($\tau o\hat{v}$ $\alpha\grave{\iota}\omega\nu\acute{\iota}ov$ $\Theta\epsilon o\hat{v}$).

Marginal references:
1 Cor. ii. 10, 11.
Gen. i. 1—26; Prov. viii. 22—31; Col. i. 16, 17.
John xvi. 13; 1 Tim. iv. 1; Rev. i. 10, 19.
Job xxxviii. 4—11.
Isa. xlvi. 9, 10.
Heb. ix. 14.
Rom. xvi. 26.
Jer. xvii. 10.

___

* The word *search*, as used in Scripture, does not necessarily imply that successive acquisition of knowledge which belongs to a finite being: for example, Jehovah says, "I the Lord search the heart."

† *See* Note at end of Chapter.

But indeed this doctrine follows from the very immutability of God. Essentially the Spirit proceedeth from the Father and the Son : He is the Spirit of our Father; he is the Spirit of his Son. Now as the very name the Eternal Father implies the Eternal Son, so if it be now that the Spirit proceedeth from the Father and the Son, it must have been from everlasting and will be to everlasting. For it is true of his immutable essence as of his unchanging love, " Thou art the same and thy years shall have no end :" " I am Jehovah, I change not :" " Jesus Christ is the same yesterday, to-day, and for ever."

Matt. x. 20.
Gal. iv. 6.

Psa. cii. 27.
Mal. iii. 6.
Heb. xiii. 8.

He is Omnipotent. The proof of this is transparent from his being associated with the Father and the Son in the creation of the worlds and of man, and from that which is more peculiarly his own office, the new creation of the soul in the image of God. He does that which Omnipotence alone can do. Therefore he is omnipotent. But, as this rather appertains to the next section, let us at once proceed to the last and most momentous attribute of Deity.

He is absolutely, infinitely, perfectly Holy and Good. I say this is the most momentous of all Divine attributes, for how little would mere omnipotence, omnipresence, omniscience, eternity, almightiness avail, dissociated from the living idea of goodness. But his name is distinctively, " The Holy Spirit." Thus David prays, " Take not thy Holy Spirit (רוּחַ קָדְשְׁךָ or ' the Spirit of thy holiness') from me." Thus Isaiah witnesses, " They rebelled and vexed his Holy Spirit (רוּחַ קָדְשׁוֹ or ' the Spirit of his holiness') ;" and asks, " Where is he that put his Holy Spirit within him?" And in the New Testament he bears this emphatic name, " The Holy Ghost," or " The Holy Spirit " (τὸ Πνεῦμα τὸ ἅγιον), no less than ninety-three times. In like

Psa. li. 11.

Isa. lxiii. 10, 11.

54　　*The Godhead of the Holy Spirit*

Psa. cxliii. 10.　manner David says, "Thy Spirit is good" (טוֹבָה):
Neh. ix. 20.　and we read in Nehemiah, "Thou gavest thy good
Spirit (רוּחֲךָ הַטּוֹבָה) to instruct them." He is so
called, as being himself essentially holy and good, and
as being to others the fountain-spring of holiness and
goodness. And when we remember that in this absolute sense it is written, "There is none good but
Matt. xix. 17.　one, that is God:" and again, "Thou only art holy,"
Rev. xv. 4.　we can only acknowledge that this is the very nature
and property of Deity. "Thou art good and doest
good." Let us proceed then to consider,

2. The Holy Spirit's acts are the actings of Godhead.

He is the Creator of heaven and earth. We all feel
the power of Paley's argument as summed up in his
own strong words, "Upon the whole after all the
schemes and struggles of a reluctant philosophy, the
necessary resort is to a Deity. The marks of design
are too strong to be gotten over. Design must have
had a designer. That designer must have been a
person. That Person is God." Or in the words of a
greater than Paley, "The invisible things of Him from
the creation of the world are clearly seen, being understood by the things that are made, even his eternal
Rom. i. 20　power and Godhead." Yet is this creation and fashion-
ing of the universe again and again ascribed to the
Holy Ghost. "The Spirit of God moved upon the
Gen. i. 2.　face of the waters." "By his Spirit he hath garnished
Job xxvi. 13,　the heavens." "The Spirit of God hath made me."
& xxxiii. 4.　"By the word of the Lord were the heavens made, and
Psa. xxxiii. 6.　all the host of them by the Spirit (רוּחַ) of his mouth."
And to these let it suffice to add the sublime challenge
of the prophet, "Who hath measured the waters in
the hollow of his hand, and meted out heaven with the
span, and comprehended the dust of the earth in a

measure, and weighed the mountains in scales and the
hills in a balance? Who hath directed the Spirit of the
Lord, or being his counsellor hath taught him?" He *Isa. xl. 12, 13.*
who made all things is God.

He holds the issues of life and death in his hands.
If there is one thing more than another which God
claims as his own prerogative, it is this, " God, that
made the world and all things therein . . giveth to
all life and breath and all things." Yet herein the *Acts xvii. 24,*
immediate agency is that of the Almighty Spirit. *25.*
" Thou sendest forth thy Spirit: they are created." *Psa. civ. 30.*
And again, " All flesh is grass . . the grass withereth,
the flower fadeth; because the Spirit of the Lord
bloweth upon it." In whom, if not in God, do we thus *Isa. xl. 6, 7.*
live and move and have our being?

He is the Author and Finisher of spiritual life.
He quickens the soul to life: this is God's prerogative: *Psa. cx. 3;*
but no one enters the kingdom who is not " born of *Acts xvi.*
the Spirit."   *14.*
   John iii. 3—8.

He dwells in the heart as in his temple: this is God's
prerogative: but we read, " Your body is the temple *2 Cor. vi. 16.*
of the Holy Ghost, which is in you."   *1 Cor. vi. 19.*

He produces celestial fruits in man: this is God's
prerogative: but it is written, " The fruit of the Spirit *Hosea xiv. 8.*
is in all goodness, and righteousness, and truth."   *Ephes. v. 9;*
   compare
He educates the children of the kingdom: this is *Gal. v. 22,*
God's prerogative: but our Lord promises, " The Com- *23.*
   Isa. liv. 13.
forter shall teach you all things . . the Spirit of truth
shall guide you into all truth." Yes, he is THE COM- *John xiv. 26,*
FORTER. What a world of thought is condensed in *and xvi. 13.*
this name. A comforter,—it is a delicate and difficult
office among men: often requiring rare tact, nice
discrimination, a firm and yet a gentle hand, a per-
suasiveness and a patience, a solicitude and a sympathy
that might tax the noblest powers. An infant's sorrow

indeed is easily assuaged; but let a few years pass, and you may try, and haply try in vain, to chase the sadness of a thoughtful child. The troubles of impulsive and impassioned youth often present a harder task. But life has deeper sorrows, the strength of manhood's grief, the anguish of a mother's bosom, the hardly wrung tears of old age. Who has not been baffled here? The heart you seek to bind up still aches on. The wound you fain would close still bleeds inwardly. Yet I grant you there are some whose vocation it seems to be to cheer and comfort others: they move among their fellows like the Good Samaritan, pouring oil and wine into stricken souls: no home ever receives them but a track of brightness is there. But such characters are few; and the sufferers are many. And there are sorrows that no human skill has ever touched, anguish of conscience, bitterness of soul, remorse for the irrecoverable past. Who of men would propose himself as a comforter for all mourners in all lands? Ere he had waded a foot-breadth into the tide of grief, he would be beyond his depth. Yet here is One who has all tender counsel and consolation for all who apply to him. Is not this the prerogative of Jehovah? " I, even I, am he that comforteth you." This office demands omniscience, omnipotence, omnipresence, eternity: and he who fulfils it must needs be " the God of all comfort."

Isa. li. 12.

2 Cor. i. 3.

This blessed Comforter prepares the soul afore unto glory: this is God's prerogative: but this in the Divine economy is the especial office of the Holy Ghost, for, " We all with unveiled face beholding in a glass the glory of the Lord are changed into the same image from glory to glory as by the Lord the Spirit."

Rom. ix. 23.

2 Cor. iii. 18.

He it is who inspired the sacred writers of the Old and New Testaments: this is God's prerogative: but

1 Tim. iii. 16.

to adduce one Scripture out of many (for the proof of this truth as given at length, see the following chapter), " Holy men of God spake as they were moved by the Holy Ghost." 2 Pet. i. 21.

He it is who anoints the Incarnate Word. For this subject treated at length see the fifth chapter of this treatise. Here let it suffice to say that the might in which the man Christ Jesus acted is ever represented in Scripture as the might of God. That might is the power of the Holy Ghost: for, " The Father giveth not the Spirit by measure unto him." John iii. 34.

And lastly, He it is who guides and governs the universal Church. For proof of this, I need but again refer to the record of his jurisdiction as contained in the Acts of the Apostles. He distributes gifts severally to every man as he wills. He ordains ministers. He shuts the door and no man opens it. He opens, and no man shuts. He rules as Master and Lord in the house of God which is the Church of the living God. 1 Tim. iii. 16

Seeing then that the Holy Spirit is the Creator of heaven and earth, that he holds the issues of life and death in his hands, that he is the Author and Finisher of spiritual life, that he inspired the sacred writers of the Old and New Testaments, that he anoints the Incarnate Word, and that he guides and governs the universal Church; we acknowledge that these are the operations of God alone, and that he who performs them can be none other than Jehovah.

3. The Divine Spirit is regarded and spoken of as God in Holy Writ.

This appears from the comparison of Scripture with Scripture. I only select a few passages out of very many. In Genesis vi. 3, we read, " Jehovah said, My Spirit shall not alway strive with man," and in 1 Pet. iii. 20, " The long-suffering of God waited in the days of Noah." Therefore we conclude, the Spirit with whom they strove was God. In 2 Sam. xxii. 2, 3, we read, " The Spirit of Jehovah spake by me and his word was in my tongue: the God of Israel said, the Rock of Israel spake to me." Therefore we conclude, the Spirit of Jehovah who spoke to David was the God and the Rock of Israel. In Acts i. 16 and xxviii. 25, we read of the Holy Ghost speaking by the mouth of David and Isaiah ; and in Luke i. 68—70 it is written, " The Lord God of Israel . . spake by the mouth of his holy prophets which have been since the world began." Therefore we conclude that the Holy Ghost is the Lord God of Israel. In Acts v. 3, 4, St. Peter says to Ananias, " Why hath Satan filled thine heart to lie to the Holy Ghost ? . . thou hast not lied unto men but unto God." Therefore we conclude the Spirit to whom Ananias and Sapphira lied was God. These passages might be greatly multiplied. The evidence they afford is constructive but most conclusive.

4. The Holy Ghost is associated with the Father and the Son in glory and worship, where the association of the creature with the Creator would confound the infinite distinction which subsists between them.

We see this in the mission, ministry, and atoning sacrifice of the Lord Jesus Christ. No one but a Divine Being could share the counsels of Jehovah in sending the Saviour into the world ; and yet we read, " From the time that it was, there am I ; and now the Isa. xlviii. 16. Lord God, and His Spirit, hath sent me." No one but a Divine Being could have enabled the Christ for his unparalleled ministry ; and yet we read, " The Spirit of the Lord God is upon me because the Lord hath ch. xli. 1. anointed me to preach good tidings," etc. No one but a Divine Being could have poured the unction of his grace upon that offering for the sins of the world ; and

yet we read, " Christ through the Eternal Spirit offered
himself without spot to God." Can you imagine any Heb. ix. 14.
angel or man taking this part? It is impossible. He
who fulfils it must needs himself be God.

Further, we see this from the Spirit's work on and
in the believer. Jesus said, " I will pray the Father
and he shall give you another Comforter that he may
abide with you for ever." And yet, who but God can John xiv. 16
dwell in the heart? as our Lord almost immediately
proceeds to speak of himself and his Father thus indwelling in the obedient disciple, " If a man love me
he will keep my words; and my Father will love him,
and we will come to him and make our abode with
him." Here the Spirit of truth, the Father, and the ch. xiv. 23.
Son alike abide in the saint. So is the sanctification
of the Spirit interwoven as a necessary link in that
heavenly chain which stretches from election to glory.
" God hath from the beginning chosen you, writes
St. Paul, unto salvation, THROUGH SANCTIFICATION OF
THE SPIRIT and belief of the truth whereunto he called
you by our gospel unto the obtaining of the glory of
our Lord Jesus Christ." And to this agree the words 2 Thess. ii.
of St. Peter, " Elect according to the foreknowledge of 13, 14.
God the Father THROUGH SANCTIFICATION OF THE SPIRIT
unto obedience and sprinkling of the blood of Jesus
Christ." Here it is enough to ask, Could the work of 1 Pet. i. 2.
any created being be thus introduced as an indispensable link in our salvation? So in the life of the
soul to Godward, St. Jude charges us, " But ye, beloved, building up yourselves on your most holy faith,
PRAYING IN THE HOLY GHOST, keep yourselves in the
love of God, looking for the mercy of our Lord Jesus
Christ unto eternal life." St. Paul affirms that, Jude 20, 21.
" Through Him (Christ Jesus) we have access BY ONE
SPIRIT unto the Father," and comforts us with the

assurance that "THE SPIRIT ITSELF beareth witness with our spirit that we are the children of God, and if children then heirs, heirs of God and joint-heirs with Christ." Is it conceivable that the co-operation of any creature should be thus requisite for prayer, and access to God, and the heart's rest on his paternal love? And thus in the great and glorious hope of our resurrection is the Holy Spirit represented as taking a consentient and co-operating part and share. " If the Spirit of him that raised up Jesus from the dead dwell in you, he that raised up Christ from the dead shall also quicken your mortal bodies by his Spirit that dwelleth in you."

Ephes. ii. 18;
Rom. viii.
16, 17.

Rom. viii. 11.

Again, the co-ordinate glory of the Holy Spirit appears as One of Three, who are Three in One, when we place side by side the two following passages.

1. There are diversities of gifts, but THE SAME SPIRIT.	1. There is one body and ONE SPIRIT, even as ye are called in one hope of your calling;
2. And there are differences of administrations, but THE SAME LORD.	2. ONE LORD, one faith, one baptism;
3. And there are diversities of operations, but it is THE SAME GOD which worketh all in all.—1 *Cor.* xii. 4—6.	3. ONE GOD and Father of you all, who is above all and through all and. in you all.— *Ephes.* iv. 4—6.

Here evidently the dignity of the Divine Spirit stands at an INFINITE distance above that of any created being whatsoever, and is on a PERFECT LEVEL with that of the Father and of the Son.

Lastly, let us come to acts of worship and adoration. And here I would first adduce the unambiguous testimony of the great evangelistic charge, " Go ye and teach all nations, baptizing them into the name (εἰς τὸ ὄνομα) of the Father, and of the Son, and of the Holy Ghost." And on this I cannot do better than quote the words of that great theologian, John Owen : " Two things these words may and do intend, nor anything else but what may be reduced unto them : first our religious owning the Father, Son, and Holy Ghost in all our Divine worship, faith, and obedience. Now as we own and avow the one so we do the other; for we are alike baptized into their name, equally submitting to their authority, and equally taking the profession of their name upon us. If then we avow and own the Father as a distinct Person, so we do the Holy Ghost. Again, by being baptized into the name of the Father and of the Son, and of the Holy Ghost, we are sacredly initiated and consecrated, or dedicated unto the service and worship of the Father, Son, and Holy Ghost. This we take upon us in our baptism. Herein lies the profession of all our faith and profession, with that engagement of ourselves unto God which constitutes our Christianity. This is the pledge of our entrance into covenant with God and of our giving up ourselves unto him in the solemn bond of religion. Herein to conceive that any one who is not God as the Father is, who is not a Person as he is also, and the Son likewise, is joined with them for the ends and in the manner mentioned, without the least note of difference as to Deity or personality, is a strange fondness destructive of all religion and leading the minds of men towards Polytheism. And as we engage into all religious obedience unto the Father and Son herein, to believe in them, trust, fear, honour and serve them, so we do the same with respect unto the Holy Ghost; which how we can do, if he be not as they are, no man can understand."*

---

* Owen on the Holy Spirit, chap. iii. sec. 14.

The benediction at the close of the second epistle to the Corinthians affords not less conclusive evidence. "The grace of the Lord Jesus Christ, and the love of God, and the communion of the Holy Ghost be with you all." It is of the nature of an indirect prayer. The blessings besought are of the highest and divinest excellence. The source whence they flow is the Triune Jehovah. The meaning of the words "the communion of the Holy Ghost" (ἡ κοινωνία τοῦ ἁγίου Πνεύματος) becomes clearer if we compare it with the parallel ex‑

1 Cor. i. 9. pression in the first epistle. Ye were called into the communion of his Son (εἰς κοινωνίαν τοῦ υἱοῦ αὐτοῦ). It implies imparted life and power and goodness. No higher blessing could be implored. And he who vouchsafes it must needs be the God of all grace.

Phil. iii. 3. On the expresssion "Who worship the Spirit of God," see note ch. i. p. 32.

So, likewise, in the opening benediction of the Apocalypse, is the highest spiritual good besought equally from the Eternal Father and from the seven‑fold Spirit and from the Lord Jesus Christ. "Grace be unto you and peace from (ἀπό) Him which is and which was and which is to come; and from (καὶ ἀπό) the Seven Spirits which are before the throne; and from (καὶ ἀπό), Jesus Christ, the faithful witness, the first be‑ gotten of the dead, and the Prince of the kings of the

Rev. i. 4, 5. earth." That by "the Seven Spirits before the throne" is designated the one Eternal Spirit of God in the perfections of his attributes and the multiplicity of His gifts, see the proof from the collation of Scripture with Scripture as given in the footnote below.* And

---

* The phrase is emblematical, but not the less definite and precise when compared with other Scriptures. Indeed, emblems are a kind of universal language for every age and country. After all that has been written on this subject, I feel

this being proved, we have here a distinct example of express adoration offered to the Holy Ghost co-ordinately with the Father and the Son.

---

persuaded that the word is here its own plain interpreter. The principal passages bearing on this are—

(1) " The Spirit of Jehovah shall rest on him ; the spirit of wisdom and understanding, the spirit of counsel and might, the spirit of knowledge and of the fear of Jehovah, and shall make him of quick understanding in the fear of Jehovah." I do not Isa. xi. 2, 3 think any stress can be laid on the *number* here, as the Hebrew only enumerates six, repeating the last with a preposition— (though the Septuagint distinguish seven, πνεῦμα σοφίας,— συνέσεως,—βουλῆς,—ἰσχύος,—γνώσεως,—εὐσεβείας,—adding as the seventh, πνεῦμα φόβου Θεοῦ) but on the *multiplicity* of perfections designated by various names and comprised in one, the Spirit of Jehovah.

(2) " Upon one stone shall be seven eyes." Zech. iii 9.

" Those seven ; they are the eyes of Jehovah, which run to and fro through the whole earth." The Septuagint translate the ch. iv. 10. seven in the same clause with the eyes, ἑπτὰ οὗτοι ὀφθαλμοί εἰσιν οἱ ἐπιβλέποντες ἐπὶ πᾶσαν τὴν γῆν.

(3) " And from the seven spirits which are before the throne." Rev. i. 4.

(4) " These things saith He that hath the seven spirits of God." ch. iii. 1.

(5) " And seven lamps of fire, burning before the throne, which are the seven spirits of God." Rev. iv. 5.

(6) " In the midst of the throne and of the four living ch. v. 6. creatures, and in the midst of the elders, stood a Lamb as it had been slain, having seven horns and seven eyes, which are the seven spirits of God sent forth into all the earth." (ὀφθαλμους ἑπτὰ οἵ εἰσιν τὰ ἑπτὰ τοῦ Θεοῦ πνεύματα τὰ ἀπεσταλμένα εἰς πᾶσαν τὴν γῆν.) No one can fail remarking the designed coincidence betwixt this and the Septuagint version, given above, of Zech. iv. 10.

Here we learn,

—from (3) and (5) *the distinction* to be observed between God and the seven spirits—for they are said to be before the throne. Therefore you could not identify them with the Father or the Lamb.

—from (2) and (4) and (6) the *mysterious union* betwixt God and them—for they are called the eyes of Jehovah ;

And this adoration is paid not by men only, but by the angels of glory. The *trishagion*, or threefold ascription of holiness to Jehovah, occurs once in the Old Testament and once in the New. And in both cases it is observable that Scripture affords a clue to the presence of the Son and of the Spirit as well as to that of the everlasting Father.

In the sixth chapter of Isaiah we read, " I saw the Lord sitting upon a throne high and lifted up, and His train filled the temple. Above it stood the seraphim. . . . And one cried unto another and said, Holy, Holy, Holy, is Jehovah of hosts: the whole earth is full of his glory. . . . Then said I, Woe is me! . . . for mine eyes have seen the King, Jehovah of hosts . . . Also I heard the voice of the Lord saying, Whom shall I send, and who will go for us? Then said I, Here am I, send me. And he said, Go and tell this people, Hear ye indeed, and understand not," &c. Now that God here manifested himself to the prophet by the express image of his Person, his only begotten

---

the spirits whom the Son of man hath—the eyes of the Lamb.

—from (3) again, that they denote a willing intelligence and not an abstract power—for to imagine that St. John prays to seven abstractions in parity with the Father and the Son for grace and peace is inconceivable.

That they cannot be angels is manifest, for the worshipping of angels is expressly forbidden.

Comparing, therefore, the other passages with (1)—remembering how Jesus Christ says that the Scripture " The Spirit of the Lord God is upon me " was fulfilled in himself—and knowing that " in the Oriental style the perfection of any quality is expressed by the number seven,"—we may fairly conclude this expression represents to us " this heavenly Agent, the Holy Ghost, in his own original and infinite perfection, in the consummate wisdom of his operations, and in the gracious munificence of his gifts."—*The Rock of Ages*, pp. 113, 114.

Col. ii. 18.

Isa. lxi. 1.
Luke iv. 21.

Pye Smith.

Son appears from the assurance, "These things said Esaias when he saw his (Christ's) glory and spake of him." But the message then sent is again recorded by John xii. 41. St. Paul and is prefaced by this remarkable introduction, "Well spake the Holy Ghost by Esaias the prophet." The glory of Jehovah of hosts was then Acts xxviii. revealed by Jesus Christ, and the voice of Jehovah of ^{25.} hosts was the utterance of the Holy Ghost. Here we decipher the true significance of the threefold adoration of the veiled seraphim, "Holy, Holy, Holy, Jehovah of hosts," and dimly apprehend why it was asked. "Who will go for us?"

So likewise in the fourth and fifth chapters of Revelation we have a view, couched in symbolic but most expressive language, of the celestial worship. A throne is set in heaven and One sat on the throne. It is then a question of absorbing interest who is the adorable Being, who there concentrates around himself the homage of saints and angels. So singular and sublime a revelation must needs draw the closest regards of every reverent mind. Is then the unity of the One there worshipped so simple an unity as to preclude any plurality subsisting therein? What saith the Scripture? The voice of the Son of Man was only now silent. "I overcame and am set down with my Father in his throne."* And in strict accordance with this we Rev. iii. 21. find, "Lo, in the midst of the throne . . . stood a Lamb, as it had been slain," and the universal worship ch. v. 5. 6. of heaven is addressed equally to "Him that sat on the throne and unto the Lamb for ever." But have we now reached the limit of that revealed? I humbly

---

* An evident distinction is here drawn between the throne of Christ which his people are admitted to share, and the throne of the Father, the supreme glories of which the Son alone with the Eternal Spirit partakes.

CHAP. III.

think not.   The question must press on every reflec-
tive student, what position do "the seven Spirits of
God" hold amid this tide of celestial adoration?   In
the benediction of the first chapter they mysteriously
intervene betwixt the Father and the Son, as One of
the blessed Three who are the fountain of grace and
peace.   In the third chapter, the Son of man describes
himself as having the seven Spirits of God.   In the
fourth chapter they appear as seven lamps of fire burning before the throne.   But what when next we read
of them?   "In the midst of the throne and of the four
living creatures, and in the midst of the elders, stood a
Lamb as it had been slain, having seven horns and
seven eyes, which are the seven Spirits of God sent

Rev. v. 6.   forth into all the earth."*   This implies their undivided
union with the Lamb, and yet the mission of the Comforter to the earth.   Therefore when the Lamb of God,
together with the eternal Father, received that universal homage, the sevenfold Spirit must have received it
with him.   How beautiful now appears the harmony with
the opening benedictory prayer ; and how appropriate
now the threefold cherubic adoration, "Holy, Holy,
Holy, Lord God Almighty, which was and is and is to
come."   The vision is symbolic, but it symbolizes
truth, shadowing forth the adoration of the hosts of

---

* If one passing mention only had been made of them, as of
the seven horns, we might have said these shadowed forth
perfect knowledge, as those perfect power : but the repeated and
varied way in which the seven Spirits are introduced prevents
our resting in this abstract interpretation ; and hence the
conjunction of the seven horns in this verse seems equivalent to
such expressions as " Jesus returned in the power of the Spirit
Luke iv. 14.   into Galilee," or " God anointed Jesus of Nazareth with the
Acts x. 38.   Holy Ghost and with power."   The above argument regarding
the worship of the seven Spirits is taken, with some condensa-
tion, from *The Rock of Ages*, pp. 127—130.

glory which is received on the eternal throne by the Father and by the Son and by the Holy Ghost.

These instances, the Triune name into which we are baptized, the threefold benediction invoked, the three-fold source of grace and peace, the trishagion both of the Old and New Testaments, seem to me so decisive a proof of the highest adoration being paid to the Spirit of God in parity with the Father and the Son, that I am the less anxious to adduce those evidences which are more constructive and indirect. But they are so significant and suggestive, I must not wholly pass them by. For example, compare the words of the Psalmist with those of the apostle :—

O come let us worship and bow down : let us kneel before the Lord our Maker. . . . To-day if ye will hear his voice, harden not your hearts, as in the provocation . . . when your fathers tempted me.—*Psa*. xcv. 6—9.	Wherefore, as the Holy Ghost saith, To-day if ye will hear his voice harden not your hearts as in the provocation . . . when your fathers tempted me.—*Heb*. iii. 7—9.

We may fairly conclude that the One whom the Psalmist calls upon us to worship is the same One whom he says the Israelites provoked. This One the parallel passage assures us was eminently the eternal Spirit : I say *eminently*, for I do not think these and other like Scriptures warrant us in excluding thoughts of the Father and of the Son. While establishing the personal Godhead of the Spirit, we must not forget his essential unity with the Father and the Son. To those who believe this, every simple command, " Worship God," embraces the worship of the Holy Spirit. But as it is the peculiar office of the Holy Spirit to strive with men, we may well believe that he was the One of the sacred Trinity peculiarly tempted and grieved by the Israelites, and therefore the One to whom suppli-cation is here peculiarly enjoined.

Again, compare the words of our Lord with the record in the Acts :—

Pray ye therefore the Lord of the harvest that he will thrust forth labourers into his vineyard.—*Matt.* ix. 38.	The Holy Ghost said, Separate me Barnabas and Saul for the work . . . so they being sent forth by the Holy Ghost. —*Acts* xiii. 2—4.

Here Christ himself ordains that prayer should be made to him who sends forth ministers : that this is one especial office of the Holy Ghost we learn from the Acts : and we have here our Lord's warrant for praying to the Spirit.

Again, bearing in mind that " the love of God is shed abroad in our hearts by the Holy Ghost," this too being another of his especial offices, let us ponder the following prayers :

" The Lord make you to increase and abound in love. . . . to the end he may establish your hearts unblameable in holiness before God even our Father at the coming of our Lord Jesus Christ."

1 Thess. iii. 12, 13.

" The Lord direct your hearts into the love of God and into the patient waiting for Christ."

2 Thess iii. 5.

In both these supplications we have the Father and Christ named besides the One to whom the prayer is addressed : may we not be assured that this One is especially the blessed Spirit of love ?

Such examples might be multiplied. But enough and more than enough of evidence has been adduced to establish this fundamental article of our faith. Seeing that the Holy Spirit's attributes are the attributes of Godhead—omnipresence, omniscience, eternity, almighty power, infinite goodness :—seeing that the Holy Spirit's acts are the actings of Godhead, whether we regard the creation of heaven and earth, the directing the issues of life and death, the regeneration and renewal of the soul, the inspiration of the Scriptures, the unction of Christ, or the government of the universal Church;—seeing that the Holy Spirit is regarded and spoken of, as God, in the Scriptures;—and lastly, seeing that the Holy Ghost is associated with the Father and the Son in glory and worship, where the association of the creature with the Creator would confound the infinite distinction which subsists betwixt them; we can draw no other conclusion than this, that he is One Person of the undivided Trinity, One with the Father and the Son, and himself very and Eternal God.

But if the conviction of his personality was solemn, surely that of his Deity is yet more awful and impressive. He is striving with the children of men. He dwells in the hearts of his people. He is very nigh unto us. He knows every thought. And this ever present One with whom we have to do is God, in whose hand our breath is, and whose are all our ways.

NOTE ON αἰώνιος, page 52.

So much has been rashly written and spoken regarding the word αἰώνιος, as if it were only equivalent to *long lasting*, instead of *everlasting*, that it may be well to present in a tabulated form its usage in the New Testament. It occurs seventy-one times.

Forty-two times of everlasting life (ζωὴ αἰώνιος) as the gift of God.

Twice of Jesus Christ as the Personal Eternal Life.	1 John i. 2, and v. 20.
Once of the Everlasting God.	Rom. xvi. 26
Once of the Eternal Spirit.	Heb. ix. 14.
Once of power everlasting (κράτος αἰώνιον) ascribed to God.	1 Tim. vi. 16.
Fourteen times of God's salvation and its issue, namely :—	
Everlasting habitations (αἰωνίους σκηνάς)	Luke xvi. 9.
Eternal weight of glory ; . . . things not seen eternal ; . . . a house eternal in the heavens.	2 Cor. iv. 17, 18; v. 1.
Everlasting consolation (παράκλησιν αἰωνίαν).	2 Thess. ii. 16.
Everlasting glory (δόξης αἰωνίου).	2 Tim. ii. 10; 1 Pet. v. 10
A brother in Christ, a possession for ever (αἰώνιον αὐτὸν ἀπέχῃς).	Philem. 15.
Everlasting salvation (σωτηρίας αἰωνίου).	Heb. v. 9.

Heb. ix. 12	Eternal redemption (αἰωνίαν λύτρωσιν).
ch. ix. 15.	Eternal inheritance (αἰωνίου κληρονομίας).
ch. xiii. 20.	Everlasting covenant (διαθήκης αἰωνίου).
2 Pet. i. 11.	Everlasting kingdom (αἰώνιον βασιλείαν)
Rev. xiv. 6.	Everlasting gospel (εὐαγγέλιον αἰώνιον).

Three times of duration as measured by ages :—

"The mystery which was kept secret since the world began" (μυστηρίου χρόνοις αἰωνίοις σεσιγημένου).

Rom. xvi. 25.

"Grace given us in Christ Jesus before the world began" (πρὸ χρόνων αἰωνίων).

2 Tim. i. 9.
etc.

"Life which God promised before the world began."

Tit. i. 2.

These last three passages seem best explained by, "He made the worlds" (τοὺς αἰῶνας): that is, the transition at God's fiat from the invisible and the increate to the visible and the created. Only remember that, as God, having created the worlds will never uncreate them, so having formed the ages he will never unform them. Hence the expression πρὸ χρόνων αἰωνίων by no means implies a point in duration, μετὰ χρόνους αἰωνίους, as if they would terminate and be no more. No argument can be drawn from this that αἰώνιος may denote a terminable existence.

Heb. i. 2 ;
and see also
xi. 3.

There remain seven solemn passages in which this word is used of everlasting woe or eternal judgment :—

Twice of everlasting fire (τὸ πῦρ τὸ αἰώνιον) as the portion of the wicked, both angels and men.

Matt. xviii.
8 ; xxv. 41.

Once of that "vengeance of eternal fire" which fell on Sodom and Gomorrha.

Jude 7.

Once of eternal damnation (αἰωνίου κρίσεως). Some important MSS. read ἁμαρτήματος, *guilt*; but Griesbach, Wordsworth, etc., prefer the received text.

Mark iii. 29.

Once of everlasting punishment (κόλασιν αἰώνιον).

Matt. xxv. 46.

Once of everlasting destruction (ὄλεθρον αἰώνιον).

2 Thess. i. 9.

And once of eternal judgment (κρίματος αἰωνίου), where the word may embrace the award of eternal life as well as that of the second death.

Heb. vi. 2.

If any one objects that the vengeance which fell on Sodom was temporal and not eternal, it is enough to answer that, while that judgment remains the most awful type earth has ever witnessed of "the lake of fire," the apostle's words embrace not only the destruction of the cities of the plain, but also the doom of their guilty inhabitants.

CHAPTER IV

THE HOLY SPIRIT ANOINTING THE SON OF MAN

THE Personality and the Deity of the Spirit rest, as we have seen, on most certain warrant of Holy Scripture. The truth which most naturally next invites our attention is his infinite unction of the Lord Jesus, the Christ of God. The subject is high and glorious; and yet it is one which, perhaps more than any other, admits us into the inmost shrine of Divine love. It is most humbling, most sanctifying, most ennobling. Oh that he who writes and they who read the following thoughts gleaned from the scattered notices of Holy Writ may be taught by the same blessed Spirit to contemplate and to adore this mystery of godliness.

(1) And first we must remember that the Eternal Spirit was one with the Father and the Son in those counsels of unsearchable unfathomable love, wherein the Triune Jehovah ordained that the Word, which was in the beginning with God, should be made flesh and tabernacle amongst us full of grace and truth. On this the testimony of Scripture is express. Thus the Lord, foretelling the conquests of Cyrus, says, "I, even I, have spoken; yea, I have called him; I have brought him, and he shall make his way prosperous. Come ye unto me, hear ye this; I have not spoken in

CHAP. IV.

Isa. xlviii.
15, 16.

secret from the beginning ;* from the time that it was, there am I: AND NOW THE LORD GOD AND HIS SPIRIT HATH SENT ME.† Thus, seven hundred years before his birth of the Virgin does the uncreated Word, claiming Jehovah's incommunicable glories of prescience and self-existence from everlasting, declare that his mission into our world was the consentient and concurrent will of the Father and of the Holy Ghost. So likewise, when arguing with the Jews, he asks, "Say ye of him whom the Father hath sanctified (ἡγίασε) and sent into the world, Thou blasphemest ;

John x. 36.

because I said, I am the Son of God ?" The order of the clauses implies that the sanctifying preceded the mission ; and the term seems to import the *setting apart of* the Son, secretly in the counsels of the Triune Godhead, and perhaps visibly by some voice or sign in the presence of the host of heaven, as the designated agent of our redemption. As such we may compare the truth here revealed by our Lord with the words of the second Psalm, " Yet have I set (margin, ' anointed ') my King upon my holy hill of Zion : I will declare the decree, the Lord hath said unto me, Thou art my

Psa. ii. 6, 7.

Son, this day have I begotten thee ;" and with the words of the prophet, " Seventy weeks are determined.

Dan. ix. 24.

. . . to anoint the Most Holy ;" and lastly with the words of the apostle, " It pleased *God* (εὐδόκησε, he, whose εὐδοκία it is, is not named : our translators have

---

* This clause, repeated from ch. xlv. 19, where it is without controversy the voice of Jehovah, refutes their interpretation who regard these words as the utterance of Isaiah regarding himself.

† Some would render the passage, " And now the Lord God hath sent me and his Spirit " But the Authorized Version, with which the Vulgate agrees, " Et nunc Dominus Jehova misit me et Spiritus ejus," is to be preferred. So Calvin.

supplied *the Father ;* but the expression is not re-
stricted to the First Person of the Trinity: it pleased
him who works all things after the pleasure of his own
will, the Triune God) that in him should all fulness
dwell." In this Divine predestination and designation Col. i. 19.
neither was the Father without the Son, nor the Son
without the Father, nor the Father and the Son without the Spirit. Nor in those affections of holy gratitude, which are awakened in our bosom towards him
who planned and designed our salvation before the
foundations of the world were laid, must we exclude
from our thoughts the co-operating love of the Eternal
Spirit.

(2) Secondly, we must remind ourselves that as the
Lord Jesus Christ in his human nature was born of
the Virgin Mary, so was he conceived of the Holy
Ghost, or as expressed in one clause of the Nicene
creed, " He was incarnate by the Holy Ghost of the
Virgin Mary." It is true that, with regard to the
Divine good pleasure and ordination, the human body
of the Lord Jesus is said by him to have been prepared by the Father, " A body hast thou prepared Heb. x. 5
me," and with regard to the willing assumption of our
human nature into indissoluble union with his Divine
nature, it is declared to be the act of the Son himself,
" Forasmuch as the children are partakers of flesh and
blood, he also himself likewise took part ($\mu\epsilon\tau\acute{\epsilon}\sigma\chi\epsilon$) of
the same." But with respect to the actual creation of Heb. ii. 14.
our Lord's body in the womb of the Virgin, it is again
and again ascribed to the efficient agency of the Holy
Spirit. Thus after the genealogy, St. Matthew's
Gospel opens, " Now the birth of Jesus Christ was on
this wise. When as his mother Mary was espoused
to Joseph, before they came together, she was found
with child of the Holy Ghost." And to this are added

the words of the angel to Joseph, " Thou son of David,
fear not to take to thee Mary thy wife, for that which
is conceived in her is of the Holy Ghost." And yet
more express and explicit are the words of Gabriel to
Mary, the chosen vehicle of this miracle of grace,
" The Holy Ghost shall come upon thee, and the power
of the Highest shall overshadow thee : therefore also
that holy thing which shall be born of thee shall be
called the Son of God." This mystery of mysteries we
adore but cannot explain. As Owen says regarding
it, " The curious inquiries of some of the schoolmen
and others are to be left unto themselves, or rather to
be condemned in them. For what was farther in this
miraculous operation of the Holy Ghost it seems pur-
posely to be hidden from us in that expression, 'The
power of the Highest shall overshadow (ἐπισκιάσει)
thee.' Under the secret glorious covert hereof, we may
learn to adore that holy work here, which we hope to
rejoice in and bless God for unto eternity."* Only
may our hearts be in unison with that noble doxology.
" It is very meet, right, and our bounden duty that we
should at all times and in all places give thanks unto
Thee O Lord, Holy Father, Almighty, everlasting God ;
*because thou didst give Jesus Christ thine only Son
to be born as at this time for us, who by the operation
of the Holy Ghost was made very man of the substance
of the Virgin Mary his Mother ; and that without
spot of sin to make us clean from all sin :*† therefore
with angels and archangels and the company of heaven
we laud and magnify thy glorious name, evermore
praising thee and saying, Holy, Holy, Holy Lord God
of Hosts, heaven and earth are full of thy glory : glory
be to thee, O Lord most high."

Matt. i. 18,
20.

Luke i. 35.

---

* Owen, ch. iii., sect. 13.
† Proper Preface upon Christmas Day.

(3) Thus was that meet tabernacle prepared for the
in-dwelling of the glorious Shekinah. The Word was
made flesh. Before his incarnation, in him dwelt all
the fulness of the Godhead incorporeally; thenceforth
and for ever, "in him dwelleth all the fulness of the
Godhead corporeally" (σωματικῶς). And thus not only Col. ii. 10.
was our Lord's human nature *negatively* sinless, but
was also from the very first *positively* full of all grace,
even the infinite grace of the Holy Spirit. Not that
this grace was in plenary conscious exercise during his
holy infancy and childhood and unfolding youth. It
was there, entire in existence, but not in entire exercise.
Herein the Child Christ Jesus increased in wisdom as
he increased in stature. As the faculties of his human
mind and reasonable soul expanded, so was the power
of the Holy Spirit in ever richer and riper manifestation. Thus far is asserted, "The child grew and waxed
strong in spirit (ἐκραταιοῦτο πνεύματι, *i. e.*, his human
spirit, which, as it grew in strength, was ever quickened
to the uttermost limit of its development by the Divine
Spirit), filled with wisdom : and the grace of God was
upon him." And again it is recorded of him after his
visit to the temple at the age of twelve years, "Jesus
increased in wisdom and in stature and in favour with
God and man." And yet we can assign no period, Luke ii. 40,
however early in the life of the incarnate Son, when   52.
the words were not true of him, "The Father giveth
not the Spirit by measure unto him." The rod came John iii. 34
forth from the stem of Jesse, and the branch grew out
of his roots, growing up before Jehovah as a tender
plant and as a root out of a dry ground, and from the
very beginning the Spirit of the Lord rested upon him,
the Spirit of wisdom and understanding, the Spirit of
counsel and might, the Spirit of knowledge and of the
fear of the Lord; and (even as he grew in bodily and

mental power) made him of quick understanding in the fear of the Lord. The plant grew up in seclusion, but its virtue could not be hid.

(4) And this unction of the Spirit was openly attested at the baptism of our Lord. It may be well to present the testimony of the four evangelists in one view :—

And Jesus, when he was baptized, went up straightway out of the water: and, lo, the heavens were opened unto him, and he saw the Spirit of God descending like a dove, and lighting upon him: and lo a voice from heaven, saying, This is my beloved Son, in whom I am well pleased.—*Matt.* iii. 16, 17.	Jesus . . . was baptized of John in Jordan. And straightway coming up out of the water, he saw the heavens opened, and the Spirit like a dove descending upon him: and there came a voice from heaven, Thou art my beloved Son, in whom I am well pleased.—*Mark* i. 10, 11.	. . . It came to pass, that Jesus also being baptized, and praying, the heaven was opened, and the Holy Ghost descended in a bodily shape like a dove upon him, and a voice came from heaven, which said, Thou art my beloved Son; in thee I am well pleased.— *Luke* iii. 21, 22.	John bare record, saying, I saw the Spirit descending from heaven like a dove, and it abode upon him. And I knew him not: but he that sent me to baptize with water, the same said unto me, Upon whom thou shalt see the Spirit descending, and remaining on him, the same is he which baptizeth with the Holy Ghost.—*John* i. 32, 33.

Henceforth the Spirit abode upon him, anointing him for his ministerial and mediatorial work. Not that we must "imagine any change in the nature or person of our Lord to have taken place at his baptism. The anointing and crowning are but *signs* of the official assumption of the power which the king has by a right independent of and higher than these." From everlasting the Holy Ghost was the Spirit of the Son, even as he was the Spirit of the Father. But now he openly took part in that mighty redemptive mission of the eternal Son which was the fruit of the counsels of the Triune Jehovah. To this Divine good pleasure a threefold witness was granted in the self same hour— the audible voice of the Father, the actual baptism of the Son, the visible descent of the Holy Ghost—a witness which brings the mystery of the Trinity more within the range of human recognition than any other which has been vouchsafed. The symbolic shape,

which the Holy Spirit deigned to assume, is full of
meaning and instruction for us as illustrated by other
Scriptures. It was a dove which found no rest for the
sole of her foot while the deluge was upon the earth,
but which came to Noah with an olive leaf in her
mouth when the waters were abated. The turtle-dove Gen. viii. 8—
11.
was one of the animals for sacrifice. The dove flees ch. xv. 9;
from the windy storm and tempest. The plumage of Levit. i. 14,
etc.
the dove is like burnished silver and gold. The ten- Psa. lv. 6—8.
ch lxviii. 13.
derness of its eye is proverbial. " My dove " is the Song i. 15;
bridegroom's name for the bride. The dove is easily iv. 1; v. 12.
ch. v. 1.
grieved, mourns plaintively, and loves its home. But Isa. xxxviii.
especially is it the emblem of innocence and harmless- 14; lix. 11;
lx. 8; Jer.
xlviii. 28.
ness as appears in the words of our Lord, " Be ye wise
as serpents but harmless as doves." The Holy Spirit Matt. x. 16.
alike in his gentle benignity and in his energizing
power, thus rested without measure on the Saviour.

(5) What then was the immediate effect of this
Divine unction? Was it repose? So far from this we
read, " Then was Jesus led up of the Spirit (ἀνήχθη
ὑπὸ τοῦ Πνεύματος) into the wilderness to be tempted
of the devil:" or as expressed by St. Mark, " And ch. iv. 1.
immediately the Spirit driveth (ἐκβάλλει) him into
the wilderness and he was there in the wilderness forty
days, tempted of Satan :" or as yet more explicitly noted Mark i. 12,
13.
by St. Luke, " And Jesus being full of the Holy
Ghost returned from Jordan, and was led by the Spirit
(ἤγετο ἐν τῷ Πνεύματι) into the wilderness, being
forty days tempted of the devil." It is, perhaps, not Luke iv. 1, 2
unworthy of 'remark that the same word is used of the
" thrusting forth" of labourers into the field. " Pray
ye therefore the Lord of the harvest, that he would
send forth (ἐκβάλῃ) labourers into his harvest," as is Matt. ix. 38.
here used by St. Mark for the Spirit's driving our
Lord into the wilderness: and the same word for his

ordinary leading of the children of God, " As many as
are led (ἄγονται) by the Spirit of God, they are the sons

Rom. viii. 14. of God," as is employed by St. Luke for the Saviour's
being led to be tempted.　The thought is full of
comfort for ministers in undertaking their arduous
labours, and for tempted believers in their sore conflicts.
But to return,—in that wilderness the Good Spirit,
dwelling without measure in the Christ, met the spirit
of Evil face to face.　In the power of the Holy Ghost
the Saviour for forty days repulsed the foe while un-
apparent: and when at length " the tempter came to
him," an expression which seems to imply a visible
appearance at the end of the forty days, he resisted
every temptation by the sword of the Spirit which is
the word of God.　Thrust after thrust was triumph-
antly parried by " It is written."　Nor can we doubt
that when the devil had ended all his temptation,
and angels came and ministered to our Lord, he whose
name is the Comforter and who delights to cheer the
toilworn and the tried, would pour his richest consolations into the breast of the weary Saviour.

　　(6) " Jesus returned," we read, " in the power of

Luke iv. 14. the Spirit into Galilee."　He came to Nazareth ; and,
as his custom was, he went into the synagogue on the
sabbath day, and stood up for to read.　And what was
the passage he selected ?　It was a prophecy, rich with
the promise of the Holy Spirit's unction : " THE SPIRIT
OF THE LORD GOD IS UPON ME ; because the Lord hath

Isa. lxi. 1. anointed me to preach good tidings unto the meek," etc.
and we read, " All bare him witness and wondered at
the gracious words which proceeded out of his mouth."
And again, shortly after, when he came down to Ca-
pernaum—" They were astonished at his doctrine, for

Luke iv. 22, his word was with power."　Herein was the fulfilment
32. of a yet earlier prophecy of Isaiah, " Behold my ser-

vant whom I uphold; mine elect, in whom my soul
delighteth: I WILL PUT MY SPIRIT UPON HIM." (It is
true that promises not unlike this had been vouchsafed
to judges and prophets of old for some particular
mission or revelation; but the issue here contemplated
was unspeakably more vast and beneficent, for Isaiah
continues)—" He shall bring forth judgment to the
Gentiles. He shall not cry, nor lift up, nor cause his
voice to be heard in the street. A bruised reed shall
he not break, and the smoking flax shall he not quench:
he shall bring forth judgment unto truth: he shall
not fail, nor be discouraged till he have set judgment
in the earth; and the isles shall wait for his law." Isa. xlii. 1—4,
This was the power in which he spoke. 'Thus Jehovah quoted as
                                                      fulfilled in
made his mouth like a sharp sword, and gave him for   our Lord,
                                                      Matt. xii.
a light to the Gentiles and to be his salvation unto the 17—21.
end of the earth." Thus were the words accomplished, ch. xlix. 2, 6.
" The Lord God hath given me the tongue of the
learned, that I should know how to speak a word in
season to him that is weary." Yes, in this same Divine ch. l. 4.
unction, he knew all men, and needed not that any
should testify of man; for he knew what was in man, John ii. 24,
and read alike the secret thoughts of his enemies, and 25.
the unexpressed sorrows of his disciples. Grace was Matt. xxii.
poured into his lips, because the Spirit of the Lord 18; John
                                                      xvi. 16.
rested upon him.

(7) And, as his words were spoken, so were his
miracles of love wrought in the power of the Holy
Ghost. Comparing St. Peter's testimony on the day
of Pentecost, " Jesus of Nazareth a man approved of
God among you by miracles and wonders and signs
which God did by him in the midst of you," with the Acts ii. 22.
same apostle's witness in the house of Cornelius, " God
anointed Jesus of Nazareth with the Holy Ghost and
with power," we learn what was that virtue which ch. x. 38.

abode in him without measure, and went out from him

for his mighty works of healing. So he expressly says
of his mightiest triumphs over the power of the
enemy, " I cast out devils BY THE SPIRIT OF GOD,"
(ἐν Πνεύματι Θεοῦ, Matt. xii. 28, compare Luke xi.
20, ἐν δακτύλῳ Θεοῦ), and founds on this his most
awful warning against blasphemy of the Spirit. The
enemy had indeed now come in like a flood: possessions
by evil spirits were frequent; but the Redeemer came
to Zion, and in his person, the Spirit of the Lord

lifted up a standard against the foe. It surely invests
every miracle of our gracious Lord with fresh interest
when we remember that each and all were wrought by
the power of the indwelling Spirit, and that, while we
look not now for miraculous gifts, yet with regard to
all the triumphs of spiritual grace his words have lost
none of their meaning by the lapse of eighteen hundred years, " Verily, verily I say unto you, he that
believeth on me, the works that I do shall he do also;
and greater works than these shall he do because I go

to the Father."

(8) And when at the close of his patient ministry
our great High Priest offered up his perfect sacrifice
to be a propitiation for the sins of the whole world,
" Christ," we read, " THROUGH THE ETERNAL SPIRIT
(διὰ Πνεύματος αἰωνίου) offered himself without spot

to God." His soul was made an offering for sin; yea,
in himself he exhausted the types of the burnt-offering,
the meat-offering, the peace-offering, the sin and tres-
pass-offerings: and this he did in the plenitude of the
unction of the Holy Ghost. When the fulness of the
time was come " to finish the transgression and to
make an end of sin; and to make reconciliation for
iniquity and to bring in everlasting righteousness, and
to seal up the vision of prophecy," then God anointed

the Most Holy; and he, the anointed One, Messiah, the Prince, was cut off, but not for himself. Thus he. the infinite victim, sanctified himself and gave himself for us, an offering and a sacrifice to God for a sweet-smelling savour. He died as he lived, full of the Holy Ghost. And as our souls glow with responsive love at thought of the Father's love, who gave his only Son, and of the Son's love, who gave himself, let us not forget the coequal and coeternal love of the Holy Spirit, in whose efficient power the stupendous sacrifice was made.

Dan. ix. 24, 26.

John xvii. 19; Ephes. v. 2.

(9) Once more, as the Saviour gave up his life, so he took it again the third day through the power of the Holy Ghost. I do not quote in support of this the mysterious passage of St. Peter, where he says that " Christ being put to death in the flesh, but quickened in Spirit (θανατωθεὶς μὲν σαρκί, ζωοποιηθεὶς δὲ πνεύματι; omit τῷ, with the best MSS.), therein also went and preached to the spirits in prison:" for I believe, as before stated—see foot-note, ch. i. p. 28—that here as elsewhere where our Lord's flesh and spirit are named, the reference is not to the third Person of the Holy Trinity, but to our Lord's human spirit. Nor do I ask my readers to dwell on the wondrous revelation here vouchsafed of our Lord's ministry between his death and resurrection, though I think from the word " quickened " (it is the Spirit that quickeneth), the sleepless energy of the Holy Ghost in him might be safely gathered. These are depths into which the light of Scripture shines but dimly. But the rising again of the Sun of righteousness is indissolubly connected, as with the will and ordination of the Father, so likewise with the agency and power of the Holy Ghost. Of this St. Paul certifies, as when he says—" If the Spirit of him that raised up Jesus from

1 Pet. iii. 18, 19.

Rom. i. 3, 4 ; 1 Tim. iii. 16.

the dead dwell in you, he that raised up Christ from the dead shall also quicken your mortal bodies by his Spirit that dwelleth in you." Christ not only, as the Son of God, *rose* from the dead in his own power; but, as the Son of man, *was raised* by the Father through the Spirit, the firstfruits of them that slept. And during those mysterious forty days, in which he showed himself alive after his passion by many infallible proofs, we read, " He THROUGH THE HOLY GHOST gave commandment unto the apostles whom he had chosen." The great evangelistic charge—the spring of all missionary exertion, to which all Christendom owes its Christianity—is equally due to the far-reaching love of the Spirit, as to that of the Saviour of the world and the Father of mankind. The Spirit of the Lord God abode on our risen Head.

(10) And lastly, now that he has ascended up on high, and led captivity captive, he has received infinite gifts of the Spirit for the rebellious sons of men, that the Lord God may dwell among them. See Psalm lxviii. 18. During his earthly ministry, he cried, " If any man thirst, let him come to me and drink: he that believeth on me, as the Scripture hath said, out of his belly shall flow rivers of living water." And this, we are told, " He spake of the Spirit, which they that believe on him should receive, for the Holy Ghost was not yet given, because that Jesus was not yet glorified." So ere he suffered he said to his apostles, " It is expedient for you that I go away; for if I go not away the Comforter will not come to you, but if I depart I will send him unto you." But having ascended up far above all heavens, that he might fill all things, he received that plenitude of grace for men. He received gifts that he might dispense them. Hence St. Paul, as he was moved by the Holy Ghost, expounding while

Rom. viii. 11.

John ii. 19; x. 18.

Acts i. 2.

John vii. 37 —39.

ch. xvi. 7.

he quotes the words of the Psalmist, referred to above, writes to the Ephesians, " He ascended up on high, he led captivity captive, and gave gifts unto men . . . and he gave some, apostles ; and some, prophets ; and some, evangelists ; and some, pastors and teachers ; for the perfecting of the saints, for the work of the ministry, for the edifying of the body of Christ." And Ephes. iv. 8, 11, 12. now he reigns in glory, our High Priest, who is set on the right hand of the throne of the Majesty in the heavens ; and the Scripture is fulfilled,—" Thy throne, O God, is for ever and ever : the sceptre of thy kingdom is a right sceptre : thou lovest righteousness and hatest wickedness : therefore God, thy God, HATH ANOINTED THEE WITH THE OIL OF GLADNESS above thy fellows. All thy garments smell of myrrh and aloes and cassia." Psa. xlv. 6 —8. What is this fragrant oil of gladness but the unction of the Holy Spirit on the head of our great High Priest ? It is true " We see not yet all things put under him : but we see Jesus, who was made a little lower than the angels, for the suffering of death, crowned with glory and honour." And we know the Heb. ii. 8, 9. everlasting decree shall be carried out in all the fulness of its meaning : " Thou art my Son, this day have I begotten thee. Ask of me, and I shall give thee the heathen for thine inheritance, and the uttermost parts of the earth for thy possession." Psa. ii. 7. 8.

Thus from the manger of Bethlehem to the highest throne of glory was the Christ anointed with the Spirit of God. Only let us remember that this same Divine unction, which abode on him without measure, must abide, according to the measure of each one, in his believing people. If any man have not the Spirit of Christ, he is none of his. This is as that precious ointment Rom. viii. 9. which was poured on Aaron's head, and went down to the very skirts of his garments. Herein as Christ is, so must we be. In this holy anointing is our strength both for communion with God and service among men. Was Jesus full of the Holy Ghost? We are commanded, " Be ye filled with the Spirit." Did the Spirit dwell in the sinless temple of his body? Our bodies, Ephes. v. 18. though sinful, are the temples of the Holy Ghost, that they may be a living sacrifice, holy, and acceptable to 1 Cor. vi. 19; God. Was Jesus led of the Spirit to be tempted ? We Rom. xii. 1. have the same sword of the Spirit for our conflict with the foe. Did the Spirit breathe words of divinest grace from the lips of Jesus? He himself has promised, The Spirit of your Father shall teach you what ye Matt. x. 20; ought to say. Did Jesus work his mighty works in Luke xii. 12. the power of the Holy Ghost? He promises the same John xiv. grace for every duty to which he calls. Did Jesus 12—17. suffer as anointed by the Spirit? We are assured, that happy are we when reproached for the name of Christ, for the Spirit of glory and of God resteth upon 1 Pet. iv. 14. us. And thus like our Lord may we pass through the grave and gate of death to our joyful resurrection. For he that raised up Christ from the dead shall quicken our mortal bodies by his Spirit that dwelleth in us, and bring us into his presence, where is fulness of joy, and set us at his right hand, where are pleasures for evermore.

CHAPTER V

THE SPIRIT THE AUTHOR OF HOLY SCRIPTURE

WHEN St. Paul demands, "What advantage hath the Jew? or what profit is there of circumcision?" he himself answers his weighty question. "Much every way: chiefly because that unto them were committed THE ORACLES OF GOD ($\tau\grave{a}$ $\lambda\acute{o}\gamma\iota a$ $\tau o\hat{v}$ $\Theta\epsilon o\hat{v}$)." This collective name for the Scriptures of the Old Testament is full of meaning. St. Stephen uses the same word, where he says Moses "received the lively oracles ($\lambda\acute{o}\gamma\iota a$ $\zeta\hat{\omega}\nu\tau a$) to give unto us." St. Paul speaks of "the first principles of the oracles of God;" and St. Peter says, "If any man speak, let him speak as the oracles of God:" these are the only other instances in which the word occurs in the New Testament. Now the meaning of *oracle* is plain. Hooker says, "An oracle is something delivered by supernatural wisdom." The oracles of the heathen were supposed to be the utterances of their gods, declaring secrets which man did not know, or unveiling a futurity which man could not penetrate. Here the Scriptures of the Old Testament—for it is to them, without controversy, the apostle refers—are declared to be the oracles of God—the God of truth who cannot lie, who inhabits eternity, and sees the end from the beginning. They are spoken of *collectively*, as forming a body of sacred writings altogether distinct from every other. So they are referred to by our Lord and his apostles as *the Scripture*, or *the prophecy of*

Rom. iii. 1.

Acts vii. 38

Heb. v. 12.

1 Pet. iv. 11.

Scripture (as such the appeal is made to them, "*It is written*"); or as *the law of God,* enunciating his commandments; or as *the word of God,* uttering his mind and will.

The sacred deposit of the Old Testament Scriptures was entrusted to the Jews. How true they were to their charge, let their own historian, Josephus, bear witness. He says, "They only were prophets that have written the original and earliest accounts of things, as they learned them of God himself by inspiration." And again: "How firmly we have given credit to those books of our own nation is evident by what we do: for during so many ages as have already passed, no one has been so bold as either to add anything to them, to take anything from them, or to make any change in them. But it becomes natural to all Jews, immediately and from their very birth, to esteem those books to contain Divine doctrines, and to persist in them, and, if occasion be, willingly to die for them. For it is no new thing for our captives, many of them in number, and frequently in time, to be seen to endure racks and deaths of all kinds upon the theatres, that they may not be obliged to say one word against our laws and the records that contain them; whereas there are none at all among the Greeks who would undergo the least harm on that account; no, nor in case all the writings that are among them were to be destroyed."* But we have better testimony than that of Josephus. "If we receive the witness of men, the witness of God is greater." And our risen Lord himself bears the most conclusive testimony to the integrity of the canon of the Old Testament as received by the Jews. He said to his apostles, after his resurrection, "These are the words which I spake

---

* Josephus against Apion, I., 7, 8.

unto you while I was yet with you, that all things must be fulfilled which were written in the law of Moses, and in the prophets, and in the Psalms, concerning me." This three-fold division was the ordinary Jewish classification of their sacred writings, the scribes reckoning under—

Luke xxiv. 44.

(1) *The law*, the five books of Moses.

(2) *The prophets*, the historical books, and the prophets, except Daniel.

(3) *The Psalms* (the Hagiographa), the book of Psalms, Daniel, and all the other canonical books, just as we receive them.

Here then our Lord appeals to the books of the Old Testament under those names which embraced the whole canon. And the inspired evangelist immediately adds, "Then opened he their understanding that they might understand THE SCRIPTURES"—thus designating the three divisions just named by the one holy name, the Scriptures. We are thus for ever assured that in receiving the Jewish Scriptures we are receiving the lively oracles of God. Here is the Divine seal set upon them. And further, our Lord immediately proceeds to confirm his own word by adding, THUS IT IS WRITTEN. It is difficult to over-estimate the value of this short argument for those who are unable to search more fully into the vast mass of historical evidence which confirms the canon. Here is the *imprimatur* of Christ.

Now this collection of writings, thus defined, our Lord and his apostles distinctly affirm to be the word of God, and to have been given by the inspiration of the Holy Ghost. Thus, when quoting Exod. iii. 6, Christ says, "Have ye never read that which was spoken unto you by God?" Hereby affirming that Moses truly recorded the very words of God at the bush, which form the introduction to his great mission to Israel. Again, in the 43rd verse of that same chapter

Matt. xxii. 31.

we read, " He saith unto them, How then doth David
IN SPIRIT (ἐν Πνεύματι) call him Lord ?" Or, as related
Mark xii. 36. by St. Mark, " David himself said BY THE HOLY GHOST ;"
or by St. Luke, " David himself saith in the book of
Luke xx. 42. Psalms." Thus words, which in the last reference are
spoken of as the words of David, are said to be " by the
Holy Ghost," or " in Spirit." So likewise the way in
which other psalms are quoted in the New Testament,
without attempting to explain the method of inspiration,
assert the fact in the most emphatic language. Let me
instance, " This Scripture must needs have been fulfilled WHICH THE HOLY GHOST BY THE MOUTH OF
Acts i. 16. DAVID SPAKE before concerning Judas." And again,
" Lord, thou art God . . . WHO BY THE MOUTH OF THY
ch. iv. 24, 25. SERVANT DAVID HAST SAID." And again, " Wherefore,
AS THE HOLY GHOST SAITH, To-day, if ye will hear his
Heb. iii. 7. voice." What is this but the echo of the last words of
David, " The Spirit of Jehovah spake by me, and his
word was in my tongue, the God of Israel said, the
2 Sam. xxiii. Rock of Israel spake to me ?" The words of the sweet
2, 3. Psalmist of Israel were the words of the Spirit of
Jehovah. So, comparing Isaiah vi. 9 with Acts
xxviii. 25, we learn that that which was spoken
by Isaiah the prophet was spoken by the Holy
Ghost.

Nor is there any distinction drawn betwixt one part
and another, as if one were more or less inspired than
another ; but, as Zacharias, when himself filled with
the Holy Ghost, says, " The Lord God of Israel . . .
spake by the mouth of his holy prophets which have
Luke i. 67– been since the world began." And so the apostle Paul,
70. writing to Timothy, says, " From a child thou hast
known the holy Scriptures (τὰ ἱερὰ γράμματα ; this
is a frequent designation of the Old Testament in
Josephus), which are able to make thee wise unto

salvation through faith which is in Christ Jesus." "All Scripture* (πᾶσα γραφη, or "every Scripture," *i.e.*, every portion of the τὰ ἱερὰ γράμματα, just named) is inspired by God (θεόπνευστος), and is profitable for doctrine, for reproof, for correction, for instruction in righteousness, that the man of God may be perfect, throughly furnished unto all good works." And to this agree the words of St. Peter: "No prophecy of the Scripture is of any private interpretation" (ἰδίας ἐπιλύσεως γίνεται), or rather "becomes a matter of self-interpretation." The words are often mysterious. The events foretold are often couched in symbol. Even the prophets themselves searched diligently into the meaning of their own predictions. No prophecy of the Scripture, therefore, is a thing of its own solution. Scripture must be compared with Scripture, signs and symbols with corresponding events, and prophecy with unfolding Providence under the teaching of the same Spirit. "For prophecy was never borne (ἠνέχθη, "wafted," *i.e.*, into the soul of the prophet) by the will of man; but holy men of God spake as they were borne along (φερόμενοι) by the Holy Ghost." Men spake, and thus the words retain all the individual characteristics of those who uttered them; but the inspiring breath was that of the Holy Ghost, and thus

2 Tim. iii. 15—17.

1 Pet. i. 11.

2 Pet. i. 21.

---

* Some would render the above, "Every Scripture, being divinely inspired, is also profitable," etc. But this (as Webster and Wilkinson justly say) does violence to the form of the sentence, and to the apostle's line of argument, who, having enforced his exhortation to Timothy to cleave to the Holy Scriptures by ascribing to them the loftiest of all powers, viz., as "able to make us wise unto salvation," lest he might be charged with ascribing too much to them, reminds his beloved son in the faith that every portion of them is inspired of God. The authorized version of this important text is, therefore, by all all means to be retained.

their utterances are nothing less than the oracles of the living God.

This inspiration was "in sundry portions and in divers manners" ($\pi o\lambda \nu\mu\epsilon\rho\hat{\omega}\varsigma$ $\kappa a\grave{\iota}$ $\pi o\lambda\nu\tau\rho o\pi\omega\varsigma$); but it was so full and entire that the result was "GOD SPAKE in time past unto the fathers by the prophets."

Heb. i. 1.

Sometimes, as in the historical books, the sacred historian may have been moved by God's Spirit to make diligent inquiry into human chronicles, and even to embody certain portions of them, as the genealogies, in his holy writing. Sometimes the inspired author may have earnestly desired to select the most appropriate language. Sometimes the inspiration came by dreams, when the outward senses were steeped in sleep. Sometimes it was by a waking vision, when the prophet was conscious to himself that his eyes were open on other material objects. Very often it was by an audible voice, as we read, "The word of the Lord came to me, saying." Perhaps most frequently it was the secret prompting of the Spirit of God in or upon the spirit of man. But in every case that which the sacred writer was moved to record, whether the chronicle of facts, or the narration of a dream from memory, or the description of a vision at the time of its occurrence, or the taking down of words as spoken by a heavenly messenger, seen or unseen, or the expression in writing of that which the Holy Spirit impressed on the heart— in every case the original Scripture was under the direct superintendence and governance of the Holy Spirit. God was responsible—if I may use the phrase with deep reverence—God was responsible for every word. So that the Bible, in the language of the great Locke, "has God for its author, salvation for its end, and truth, without any mixture of error, for its matter."

Eccles. xii. 10.
Job xxxiii. 14, 15.

Num vii. 8.

Jer. xx. 9.

Some have urged the futile objection that we find recorded in Scripture the sayings of misguided men, as of Job's friends, or of open sinners, as of Cain and Judas, or even .of the devil and his angels ; and they ask, not without contempt, whether these sayings were inspired ? It seems difficult to believe the objection is proposed seriously ; but a child might answer it. The words as first uttered were evil, and not inspired from above : the truthful narration of them when uttered God saw to be expedient for our instruction, and therefore moved his prophets and apostles to narrate them.

The Scriptures, then, as first written, were pure unadulterated truth. We cannot allow that there was in them the smallest grain of error. I say as first written, for I am not speaking of the superficial errors which have crept in through the inadvertence of copyists or the defect of translators. These, taking the sum of them all, are marvellously few. But the originals were perfect. This is asserted again and again : " The words of the Lord are pure words, as silver tried in a furnace of earth, purified seven times." Ps1. xii. 6. " The law of the Lord is perfect, converting the soul : the testimony of the Lord is sure, making wise the simple : the statutes of the Lord are right, rejoicing the heart : the commandment of the Lord is pure, enlightening the eyes : the fear of the Lord is clean, enduring for ever : the judgments of the Lord are true and righteous altogether." Or, in the brief ch. xix. 7—9. weighty dictum of Agar, EVERY WORD OF GOD IS PURE. And this, as we have seen, our Lord and his Prov. xxx. 5. apostles explicitly affirm, quoting without restriction the law, the Psalms, and the prophets, as the word of the living God, which abideth for ever.

The proofs hitherto adduced have especially regarded

the inspiration of the Old Testament.* We should be prepared to find an equally infallible and inspired guide

---

* The most strenuous attacks of sceptical criticism have recently been directed against the miracles, and in some cases against the morality and doctrines of the Old Testament. Some writers condescend to patronize the New Testament, who dare to impugn the veracity or the virtue of the Old. But in truth the two Testaments are inseparably connected. Not only are there about one hundred and ninety distinct and separate quotations from the Old in the New Testament—many consisting of several verses, and many repeated again and again, so that between three and four hundred verses in the New Testament are taken from the Old; but it is observable that all the most miraculous histories narrated in the Old Testament—and therefore those most con- troverted—are endorsed in the New Testament, and all the most essential doctrines of the New Testament are foreannounced in the Old.

(1) Thus with regard to the miracles of the Old Testament :—

Heb. iv. 4.	The creation in six days and the seventh day of rest.
Matt. xix. 4; Acts xvii. 26; 1 Tim. ii. 13.	The human race from one pair.
2 Cor. xi. 3; Rom. v. 12.	The temptation and fall.
Heb. xi. 5; Jude 14.	The rapture of Enoch.
Matt. xxiv. 38; 2 Pet. iii. 6.	The flood.
Acts vii. 3.	The call of Abram.
Luke xvii. 28; 2 Pet. ii. 6.	The destruction of Sodom.
Rom. iv. 19, 20; Heb. xi. 11.	The miraculous birth of Isaac.
Heb. xi. 20—22.	The prophetic benedictions of Isaac, Jacob, and Joseph.
James v. 11.	The history of Job.
Mark xii. 26; Acts vii. 30—34.	The theophany at the burning bush.
Acts vii. 36; xiii. 17; Heb. xi. 28, 29.	The miracles of the exodus, the passover, and the passage of the Red Sea.
John vi. 49; 1 Cor. x. 1—10.	The miracles in the wilderness, embracing the manna, the water from the rock, etc.
Heb. xii. 18 —21; Acts vii. 38; 2 Cor. iii. 7.	The law given from Sinai.
Jude 11.	The earthquake which swallowed Korah and his company.
John iii. 14, 15.	The brazen serpent.
2 Pet. ii. 16.	The dumb ass speaking with man's voice.

in the Scriptures of the New Covenant; and so it is. We have not, indeed, a third revelation, to certify us of the Divine inspiration of the second, as the second does of the first. This the case does neither admit of nor require; for in this way we should need a fourth to assure us of the third. But whatever proofs satisfied the Jews that Moses and the prophets spoke and wrote in God's name, we have the same and yet stronger

The fall of the walls of Jericho.	Heb. xi. 30.
The wonderful biographies of Gideon, and Barak, and Samson, etc.	Heb. xi. 32—34.
The drought and rain at Elijah's prayer.	James v. 17.
The cure of Naaman.	Luke iv. 27.
The vision of the Divine glory by Isaiah.	John xii. 41.
The narrative of Jonah.	Matt. xii. 40, 41.
The three children in the furnace, and Daniel in the lions' den.	Heb. xi. 33, 34.

If men will impugn the veracity of these Old Testament statements, they must deny that of Christ and his apostles.

And (2) All the most essential doctrines of the New Testament are foreannounced in the Old:—

The unity of the Godhead.	Deut. vi. 4; Isa. xliv. 6
The coequal Deity of the Son and of the Holy Spirit.	Isa. ix. 6; xl 13; xlviii. 6
The corruption of human nature.	Gen. vi. 5; Psa. li. 5; Jer. xvii. 9.
The atonement.	Lev. xvii. 11; Psa. li. 7; Isa. liii. 10; Dan. ix. 24, 26.
Justification by faith.	Isa. xlv. 21—25; Jer. xxiii. 6; Hab. ii. 5.
The renewal by the Holy Ghost.	Psa. li. 11; Ezek. xxxvi. 26, 27.
The infallibility and perpetuity of God's word.	Psa. xii. 6; xix. 7—9; Isa. xl. 8.
The necessary fruit of good works.	Lev. xix. 2; Ezek. xviii. 5—9, etc.
The last judgment.	Psa. xcvi. 13: Eccles. xii. 14; Dan. vii. 10.
The eternal issues of that judgment.	Psa. ix. 17; Dan. xii. 1, 2
The everlasting kingdom of the Prince of Peace.	Num. xiv. 21; Psa. li. 8; Isa. ix. 6, 7.

So that, as has been well and tersely said, *In vetere Testamento novum latet, in novo vetus patet.*

evidences regarding the books of the New Testament. "God, who . . . spake in time past unto the fathers by the prophets, hath in these last days spoken unto us by his Son." Large portions of the Gospels contain the very words of the eternal Son of God, speaking in his Father's name. Were Moses and the prophets accredited by miracles? so were Christ and his apostles. Did they come supported by the ministry of angels, and announcing the visions of God? so these. Did they speak as God's ambassadors, declaring his will, foretelling future events, promising rewards, and denouncing judgments? so these. Did the elder prophets open their commission, "Thus saith the Lord?" the apostles write with equal authority, as the prefaces of all their epistles testify. St. Peter classes both together when he calls on those to whom he wrote to be "mindful of the words which were spoken before by the holy prophets, and of the commandment of us, the apostles of the Lord and Saviour;" and he places "the epistles of his beloved brother Paul" on the same level with "the other Scriptures," which the unlearned wrest. And St. Paul cites one passage from Deut. xxv. 4, and another from Luke x. 7, without distinction, and both as the authoritative written word of God: "The Scripture saith, Thou shalt not muzzle the ox that treadeth out the corn. And, The labourer is worthy of his hire."

Heb. i. 1, 2.

2 Pet. iii. 2, 15, 16.

1 Tim. v. 18.

This inspiration was only a fulfilment of the direct assurances of our Lord to his apostles. Thus he promised St. Peter and the rest, "Verily I say unto you whatsoever ye shall bind on earth shall be bound in heaven; and whatsoever ye shall loose on earth shall be loosed in heaven." To bind and to loose are, in Jewish language, to forbid and to permit. These words, therefore, certify us that what the apostles forbade as

Matt. xvi. 19; xviii. 18.

contrary to their Master's will, should be forbidden
with the authority of God, and that what they sanctioned as according to their Master's will, should be
sanctioned with the authority of God.   For, this it
need not be said, inspiration was indispensable.   And
this was the office of the promised Comforter, as testi-
fied by those august declarations of our Lord ere he
suffered, " These things have I spoken unto you, being
yet present with you; but the Comforter, which is the
Holy Ghost, whom the Father will send in my name,
he shall teach you all things, and bring all things to
your remembrance whatsoever I have said unto you."
And again, " But when the Comforter is come, whom I
will send unto you from the Father, even the Spirit of
truth which proceeded from the Father, he shall testify
($\mu\alpha\rho\tau\upsilon\rho\acute{\eta}\sigma\epsilon\iota$) of me, and ye also testify ($\mu\alpha\rho\tau\upsilon\rho\epsilon\hat{\iota}\tau\epsilon$),
because ye are with me from the beginning."   And
again, " Howbeit when he the Spirit of truth is come, he
will guide you into all truth, for he shall not speak of
himself ($\dot{\alpha}\phi'$ $\dot{\epsilon}\alpha\upsilon\tau o\hat{\upsilon}$, i. e., independently of, or contrary
to, the Father or the Son), but whatsoever he shall hear
that shall he speak, and he will show you things to
come.   He shall glorify me; for he shall receive of
mine, and shall show it unto you."   Now if this Divine
and plenary inspiration was necessary for the apostolic
preaching of the Gospel to that generation, it was of
tenfold importance for their writings, which are for all
after generations of believers; and the apostles appeal to
their writings as confirming their words, as, for example,
St. Paul writes to the Thessalonians, " Remember ye not
that when I was yet with you I told you these things?"

John xiv. 26·
xv. 26, 27;
xvi. 13, 14

2 Thes. ii. 5.

And for themselves, whether in preaching or writing,
the ambassadors of the cross claim to be heard as declaring God's truth by his authority and by the inspiration of his Spirit; as in the noble doxology which closes

the epistle to the Romans, St. Paul writes, "Now unto him that is of power to establish you according to my gospel and the preaching of Jesus Christ, according to the revelation of the mystery which was kept secret since the world began, but now is made manifest, and by the Scriptures of the prophets, according to the commandment of the everlasting God, made known to all nations for the obedience of the faith, to God only wise, be glory through Jesus Christ for ever." And this Divine authority is claimed not only for the subject-matter of their evangelical message, but for the very words in which it is conveyed. "We have received, not the spirit of the world, but the Spirit which is of God, that we might know the things which are freely given to us of God; which things we speak, NOT IN THE WORDS WHICH MAN'S WISDOM TEACHETH, BUT WHICH THE HOLY GHOST TEACHETH, comparing spiritual things with spiritual." Words so uttered or written are the very voice of God. "If any man," says the apostle in the same epistle, "think himself to be a prophet or spiritual, let him acknowledge that the things that I write unto you are the commandments of the Lord." *

Rom. xvi. 25—27.

1 Cor. ii. 13.

ch. xiv. 27.

And in the same way St. John unhesitatingly declares, "We are of God: He that knoweth God heareth us; he that is not of God heareth not us: hereby know we the spirit of truth and the spirit of error." The same authority pervades the whole New Testament, until the closing book of the canon is thus solemnly fenced: "If any man shall add unto these words, God shall add unto him the plagues that are written in this book: and if any man shall take away from the words of the book of this prophecy, God shall take away his part out of the book of life, and out of the holy city, and from

1 John iv. 6.

---

* See Note at end of Chapter.

the things which are written in this book." From a
review of the whole we may surely say, that if language
such as that employed by the sacred writers of the Old
and New Testament does not claim infallible inspiration,
no words, however exact or express, could claim it.

This inspiration is quite compatible with the clear
human characteristics which mark every page of Scripture. You could never mistake Moses' mind for
David's, or Isaiah's mind for Jeremiah's, or Peter's
mind for Paul's. They were *men* who spoke, and *men*
who wrote, but men moved by the Holy Ghost. Sometimes, indeed, they only recorded a message given to
them immediately from the mouth of the Lord; but
far more often the divinely inspired thoughts were
breathed through their own minds, and uttered in their
own words, though words prompted and superintended
by the Holy Spirit. Thus, ordinarily, they were not
mere amanuenses or penmen, but inspired authors—
authors preserved from every error, and guided into all
truth.* God speaks to us through them, not in Divine

---

* Hence I am not fond of the word *dictation*, as applied to the
inspiration of Scripture. It is not a term used in the Bible
itself, and it applies to but a small portion of the sacred volume.
The frequent employment of this word seems to me almost the
only flaw in Gaussen's masterly work " Theopneustia." But
how firmly he held the same view I advocate above appears from
the following noble illustration of the individuality of the sacred
writers :—

" Has the reader ever paid a visit to the astonishing organist,
who so charmingly elicits the tourist's tears, in the Cathedral at
Freiburg, as he touches one after another his wondrous keys, and
greets your ear by turns with the march of warriors on the river
side, the voice of prayer sent up from the lake during the fury
of the storm, or of thanksgiving when it is hushed to rest? All
your senses are electrified, for you seem to have seen all, and to
have heard all. Well then it was thus that the Lord God,
mighty in harmony, applied, as it were, the finger of his Spirit
to the stops which he had chosen for the hour of his purpose,

or angelic, but in human language. So that in truth
we often scarcely know whether to admire most the
Divinity or the humanity of Scripture; so thoroughly
human, it appeals to every sympathy within us; so
transparently divine, it is pure unadulterated truth.
The similarity here is close between the Incarnate
Word and the written word of God. In Jesus on
earth there was every sympathy with suffering, and
every sinless human weakness. He was in all things
made like unto his brethren. He wrought as a car-
penter. Hungry and thirsty, his soul fainted within
him. Wearied with his journey, he sat on Jacob's
well. He was as perfect man as he was perfect God.
So it is with the written word. It is pure and perfect.
But at times it seems to labour for thought and to
faint for expression, and to say, if we may venture to
adapt the utterance of Jesus, The time cometh when I
shall no more speak unto you in proverbs. In its
sacred characters God speaks, and man speaks. Who

---

and for the unity of his celestial hymn. He had from eternity before him all the human stops which he required: his Creator's eye
embraces at a glance this range of keys stretching over threescore
centuries; and when he would make known to our fallen world
the everlasting counsel of his redemption and the coming of the
Son of God, he put his left hand on Enoch, the seventh from
Adam, and his right on John, the humble and sublime prisoner
of Patmos. The celestial anthem, seven hundred years before
the flood, began with these words, 'Behold the Lord cometh
Jude 14.   with ten thousands of his saints, to execute judgment upon all;'
but already in the mind of God the voice of John had answered
to that of Enoch, and closed the hymn three thousand years
after him, with these words, 'Behold he cometh with clouds,
and every eye shall see him, and they also which pierced him.
Even so, Lord Jesus, come quickly. Amen.' And during this
hymn of thirty centuries, the Spirit of God never ceased to
breathe in all his messengers. . . . God's elect were moved, and
life eternal came down into the souls of men."—*Theopneustia,
translated by D. D. Scott*, ch. i. sec. v.

can lay bare the mystery? Who can dissect the mingled shadings of the colours of the rainbow?

But this inspiration of Scripture, though perfectly consistent with the individuality of the several writers, is altogether inconsistent with those rationalistic theories which subvert the faith of some in the present day. It absolutely refuses to allow the existence of anything false, or fallible, or merely human in the Scriptures as first given by God to man. Then should we need yet another revelation to assure us what was inspired and what uninspired, what was fallible and what infallible, what was human and what Divine. Further, it positively resists the theory of human reason, or any verifying faculty in man, being the ultimate judge of God's revelation. " For the prerogative of God," says Bacon, "extendeth as well to the reason as to the will of man; so that as we are to obey His law, though we find a reluctation in our will, so are we to believe His words, though we find a reluctation in our reason. For if we believe only what is agreeable to our sense, we give consent to the matter, not to the Author, which is no more than we do to a suspected and discredited witness. Nor ought we to draw down or submit the mysteries of God to our reason, but, contrariwise, to raise and advance our reason to the Divine truth."

This obedience of faith does not in the very least interfere with the useful and important duty of critical investigation. Though, in better words than my own, " Let us always be cautious that we do not extend criticism beyond its just limits. To investigate the merits of copies and versions; to lead us up by a careful process of inquiry to the very text, as near as may be, as it was penned by the various authors; to illustrate what they have said, and to facilitate the understanding of their words,—this is the object, this the ample field

of sacred criticism. But an awful responsibility is incurred if we elevate it into the judge of prophets and
apostles, to censure them for what they *have* said, and
to pronounce what they should have said; to declare
their reasoning inconclusive, and their statements in-
accurate; to regard them as led astray with false
philosophy, and bewildered for want of recollection; to
thrust them, in fact, far below a shrewd professor in a
German university, who could have taught the world
more skilfully than they did,—from this the devout
mind should intuitively shrink. We are commanded,
indeed, to prove all things: we are encouraged by the
book itself to search whether the things it tells us be
so. But surely the authenticity and general truth-
fulness of the record being established, its own testimony
is sufficient to vindicate its highest claims."*

These claims—to sum up what I have said before—are
nothing less than the plenary inspiration of Scripture,
from Genesis to Malachi, from Matthew to Revelation.
Every jot and tittle of the Bible, as originally penned
by the sacred writers, is GOD's WORD WRITTEN—I repeat,
as originally penned, for the truth here affirmed does
not ask us to believe in the inspiration of copyists or
translators or interpreters. Superficial errors, though
we believe them to be few and comparatively unim-
portant, may have crept in during the lapse of ages.
But the autographs were perfect. They may record
the ungodly sayings and sentiments of ungodly men,
but those sayings are historically true, and it was the
mind of the Spirit thus to record them. They may
embody earlier uninspired documents; but, if it be so,
the fact of the Holy Ghost moving the sacred writers
to embody them proves that every word is true, and

---

* Ayre's Introduction to Biblical Interpretation, pp. 306, 307.

stamps every sentence thus taken into the canon of Scripture with the seal of God. They do in their various parts bear the unmistakable impress of the individual character of every author (for inspiration is not of necessity dictation), but each one spake as he was moved by the Holy Ghost. So the one inspiring breath of the organ gives forth the sound, which the conformation of every pipe impresses on it. It is God speaking to man in man's language. And as the Incarnate Word was subject to the innocent infirmities of humanity, though absolutely and perfectly without sin, so the written word is the mind of God, couched in the feeble symbolism of human speech, but yet is pure, perfect, and infallible. This glorious possession—this choicest heirloom of the family of man—we owe to the inspiration of the Holy Ghost.

NOTE ON 1 Cor. vii. 12, 25, 40.—Some serious students have felt such difficulty in St. Paul's statements, 1 Cor. vii. 12, 25, 40, that I venture to add some extracts from my "Commentary on the New Testament," which are mainly gleaned from Lee's valuable work on Inspiration :—

Vers. 6—11. *But I say this by way of allowance* (κατὰ συγγνώμην), *not by way of command—i. e.*, an allowance conceded to you. "As Olshausen observes, συγγνώμη differs from γνώμη (ver. 25) only so far as the 'judgment' of the apostle comprises here the additional notion of 'a concession.'"—(*Lee.*) St. Paul would gladly have heard that all those who had sought his counsel in this matter (such seems the force of "*all men*," ver. 7) had been able to live unmarried as contentedly as himself, during that time of "present distress" and of strenuous labour in the first planting of the churches of Christ. But he knew that this could not be, for the temperaments of men, as ordained by God himself, differed one from the other (see Matt. xix. 10—12). Therefore, speaking as he was moved by the Holy Ghost, he said, let the unmarried, if they had the gift of continency, remain in celibacy ; if not, let them marry, for this was far better than to be consumed with desires which might lead them into sin. With respect to those already married, it was not necessary for the apostle to give any new

1 Cor. vii.

direction—the Lord Jesus had expressly decided the matter when he solemnly ratified the original law of marriage (Mark x. 12). Therefore, *Let not the wife be separated from her husband ; but if she is already separated* (χωρισθῇ), etc. " This supposes a case of *actual* separation, contrary to Christ's command ; if such have really (καί) taken place, the additional sin of a new marriage must not be committed, but the breach healed as soon as possible."— (*Alford*.) *And let not the husband put away his wife,* with the one exception, of course, allowed by Christ himself (Matt. xix. 9).

Vers. 12—17. *But to the rest speak I, not the Lord*—not that the following decision is uninspired, or less binding than the former ; but the Lord, when on earth, not having uttered express directions regarding such cases, now commissioned St. Paul to give his inspired judgment. " All supposed distinction between the apostle's own writing ' *of himself* ' and ' *of the Lord* ' is quite irrelevant. He NEVER wrote ' *of himself* ' [at least, in his canonical epistles], being a vessel full of the Holy Ghost, who ever spoke by him to the church."—(*Alford*.) The inference that, in certain parts of Scripture, the author may write according to his own uninspired judgment, although guided in other portions of his work by the Holy Ghost, is altogether at variance with St. Paul's design ; and his words can only be distorted into the form of an argument against inspiration by utterly overlooking his object and his meaning. The words (ver. 10), " I command, yet not I, but the Lord," obviously refer to the re-institution by Christ of the original law of marriage, and relate to an ordinance, revealed from the very first, which is obligatory in every age. In the passage (vers. 10—17) prefaced by " To the rest speak I, not the Lord," the very nature of the question, which arose from the transitional state of society then existing, explains why our Lord had not himself promulgated an express law respecting it. Here, as in other matters of discipline, the Holy Ghost was to guide the apostles into " all the truth ;" and the decisions, therefore, at which they arrived are equally binding with those of Christ himself. This is clear from St. Paul's own words when summing up the question, *So ordain I in all the churches.* Again, when he writes (ver. 25), " Concerning virgins I have no commandment of the Lord, yet I give my judgment," etc., he alludes to the fact that Christ, when laying down his commands, had made no provision for this special exigency ; and, consequently, St. Paul proceeds here also to pronounce his " judgment," introducing his decision with the words, " I suppose (or, rather, consider) that this is good for the present distress." The *command-*

ment of the Lord does not signify the inward suggestion of the Holy Ghost; but, as above explained, an express utterance of Christ when on earth. So far, indeed, was the apostle from intending to convey by these words the idea that any of his inspired directions to the church were to be looked upon as of less authority than even those of Christ himself, that in this same epistle, having referred to the existence of special miraculous gifts in the church (of which a prominent gift was the faculty of " discerning of spirits "), he appeals to persons thus endowed in the remarkable words, " If any man think himself to be a prophet, or spiritual, let him acknowledge that the things that I write unto you are the commandments of the Lord," ch. xiv. 37.

And again :—

Ver. 25—40. *Now concerning virgins* (παρθένων—*i. e.*, the unmarried of both sexes: see Rev. xiv. 4—*Bengel*), etc. On the subject of celibacy, whether it were expedient or not during such a season of necessity as was then pressing on the Corinthian church, the apostle had no express command of Christ, given when he was on earth, to hand down to them, but proceeds to give his own inspired counsel. *I suppose* (νομίζω)—no uncertainty lurks in this word; it is the deliberate judgment of one taught by the Holy Ghost—*that this is good for the present distress*—persecution being imminent, and this at a time of widespread famine, and of pestilences in divers places.

The last two verses regulate, on the same principles, the marriage of widows. They are free to marry—with one solemn proviso, that it be *in the Lord*—but are happier if they remain unmarried, according to the apostle's judgment, to which he adds the seal of his own inspiration, *I wot that I too have the Spirit of God.* This clause rebukes any doubt or questioning of the fact.

CHAPTER VI

THE SPIRIT STRIVING WITH THE WORLD

WE have seen how the Personality and Deity of the
Holy Ghost alike rest on the sure testimony of the
word of God. We have dwelt on that infinite unction
of his grace which abode in the Son of Man. We have
considered that Divine inspiration which breathes in
the living oracles of Holy Writ. The way is now open
to us humbly and reverently to trace the workings of
this same Eternal Spirit in the heart of man. And
that which may first most suitably engage our attention is his striving with the world, even with those
who finally and for ever resist his gracious influences.

That such resistance is possible, appears both from
Scripture and experience. Let it here suffice to appeal
to two passages, one from the Old, the other from the
New Testament.

Of the world before the flood, when all flesh was
beginning to corrupt its way upon the earth, we read,
"Jehovah said, My Spirit shall not always strive (יָדוֹן)*
with man, for that he also is flesh; yet his days shall
Gen. vi. 3. be an hundred and twenty years." The verse might
be thus paraphrased, "My Spirit shall not always

---

* The Hebrew word *yadon* signifies "judge," or "strive in
judgment;" as in Eccles. vi. 10, "Neither may man contend
(דִין) with him that is mightier than he." Compare Job. xix. 29,
where דִין is rendered "judgment."

strive with man, in whom the flesh thus overcomes and overbears the Spirit, but being resisted, and grieved and provoked, will leave the ungodly to themselves at length, though a respite shall be granted of an hundred and twenty years ere the judgment fall." In what way the Spirit contended with man is not expressly revealed; but we may argue from analogy, that he strove as now by the witness of creation, wherein his eternal power and Godhead are clearly seen, by the actings of his Providence distinguishing the sinner and the saint, and by the voice of his umpire conscience within. Further, the world then had the testimony of those (such as Noah's father, Lamech) who had known Adam; and Adam had known and talked with God. Again, many think the guard of the cherubim was not removed from Eden's gate until the flood. Then, doubtless, the sacrifices of the righteous, like that of Abel, were accepted; and the prayers of those who called upon the name of the Lord brought answers of peace. Then Enoch Gen. iv. 26. walked with God, and endured the contradiction of sinners, and was translated that he should not see death. But especially we may suppose the Spirit strove by the godly life and preaching of Noah, that great preacher of righteousness, and who alike by his words and deeds proclaimed his belief in the coming deluge, and thus condemned the disobedient world. The combined force thus brought to bear upon the rebellious wills of the children of men—a force wielded by the Holy Spirit himself—must have been very powerful. We can well believe that it grappled with many consciences. Probably some trembled, and some were almost persuaded. But the mournful issue was, Noah and his family alone entered the ark: the rest perished in the flood of waters.

The second instance I would adduce is yet more

solemnly impressive. St. Stephen, ere he sealed his testimony with his blood, thus faithfully warned the
Sanhedrim before whom he stood: " Ye stiff-necked
and uncircumcised in heart and ears, ye do always
resist (ἀντιπίπτετε)* the Holy Ghost : as your fathers

Acts vii. 51. did, so do ye." Those to whom St. Stephen spoke
were the leaders of Israel, the chosen priests and
elders of the chosen nation, that nation which for nearly
two thousand years had been the channel of God's
grace in a fallen world. That generation was the last
in a series distinguished from age to age by ever fresh
gifts of Divine bounty. They were possessed of price-
less heirlooms, which had been accumulating for near
twenty centuries; for they were Israelites to whom
pertained the adoption, and the glory, and the cove-
nants, and the giving of the law, and the service of
God, and the promises. And not only were they the
possessors of all this hereditary excellence ; but far
more—in their days the fulness of time had come.
The great forerunner had preached in the spirit and
power of Elijah. And at last the Son of God himself
had come and tabernacled amongst them, and had
spoken as never man spake, and wrought works such
as man never did, and had suffered, and died, and risen
again, and ascended to glory, attested both by angels
and men, and according to his sure promise had sent
down the Holy Ghost from heaven, a mighty and
visible baptism of fire. And now for six years† had

* ἀντιπίπτω, here only in the New Testament: compare
Num. xxvii. 14, "in the strife (ἐν τῷ ἀντιπίπτειν, LXX.) of the
congregation." The image is that of waves hurled upon a rock,
or bands of armed men throwing themselves on an advancing
phalanx.

† According to the best chronologists, six years and two
months seem to have intervened betwixt our Lord's crucifixion
and the death of Stephen.

the commission, entrusted to the apostles, been ratified and confirmed with signs and wonders and miraculous gifts of the Spirit. Multitudes had repented. A great company of the priests were obedient to the faith. But Israel, as a nation, was obdurate ; and their council only too faithfully represented the unbelief of the people. Stephen was arraigned. He was filled with the Holy Ghost. A light from heaven shone upon his face. In a wondrous review of God's dealings he traced the parallel betwixt Moses and a greater than Moses. All was of no avail. The indignation of his audience was on the point of bursting forth. And seeing that only a few minutes longer remained to him, he with unflinching courage charged them with this awful sin, a sin in which they were filling up the measure of their fathers, " Ye do always resist the Holy Ghost."

These words afford the most solemn proof of man's tremendous responsibility :—the Holy Ghost was resisted, and resisted successfully. But is he not Almighty? It is enough to point to that creation, which is his work, to answer, Yes:—and this not an impersonal influence, or fatal force, which, however vast, we would perhaps imagine the quick intelligence of the human spirit to evade or defy. But is he not himself an intelligent Being, a Divine Person, of infinite wisdom and goodness and love as well as power? The Scriptures, as we have seen, abundantly prove that he is. How then shall man, puny man, the creature of a day, resist this Almighty One? Will not this Omnipotent Creator drag his creature captive at his chariot wheels? Here we can only answer, He worketh all things after the counsel of his own will. IPSE VULT NOS VELLE. There is no discord in the Divine mind. The counsel of the Triune Jehovah, that shall stand. He will not suffer the laws of his spiritual kingdom to be violated. And the Father, the Lord of heaven and earth, hides from the wise and prudent that which he reveals to babes. We can only echo the words of Jesus Christ, " Even so, Father, for so it seems good in thy sight." It is not for us to penetrate those secret things which belong to the Lord our God. But it is ours with fear and trembling to learn the solemn lesson, which is taught us alike by the world before the flood and by the Jews of the apostolic age, that the omnipotent and omnipresent Spirit, while he persuades some among the children of men by his grace to embrace the truth, is by others resisted finally, fatally, and for ever.

Seeing then that the fact is clearly stated in the word of God, it surely becomes us patiently and prayerfully to inquire, what further light is therein vouchsafed on the Holy Spirit's striving with those who are nominally within the pale of the Church, but who resist his saving grace to the last and perish in their sins. I would restrict the question to those professedly within the pale of the Church or in immediate contact with its members. The further inquiry, how far the Holy Spirit works upon those without, in heathen lands, is a profound depth, upon which all who think at all have probably thought much, but which, being rather a matter of speculative theology, whereon very few and scattered rays of revelation fall, lies beyond the range of this treatise.

Confining then our researches to those who dwelt under the influences of the Old Covenant, or who dwell under the shadow of the New, we must remember,

(1) *It is the Holy Ghost who enlightens the understanding.* " Every good gift and every perfect gift is from above and cometh down from the Father of lights." His good pleasure is effected by his eternal

Matt. xi. 25, 26.

James i. 17.

Word and Spirit. We see this in the material creation. Gen. i. 1;
John i. 2;
Isa. xl. 12,
13.
So is it in the world of spirit. God who commanded
the light to shine out of darkness shines in the hearts
of his children to give the light of the knowledge of
the glory of God in the face of Jesus Christ. Christ 2 Cor. iv. 6.
is the true light which lighteth every man that cometh
into the world. And the Spirit of truth from the John i. 9.
beginning, and more especially in this his ministration,
glorifies Christ. But this gospel light shines on many cb xvi. 14;
1 Cor. iii. 8.
who do not comprehend it. Their understanding is John i. 5.
illuminated, but their soul is not quickened. And so
we are solemnly warned that those who have been
enlightened ($\phi\omega\tau\iota\sigma\theta\acute{\epsilon}\nu\tau\epsilon\varsigma$) may yet fall away. Heb. vi. 4—6.

(2) *It is the Holy Ghost who convicts the world of
sin, righteousness, and judgment.* The well-known John xvi. 8—
11.
words from our Lord, to which I here refer, embrace
a conviction unto condemnation, and a convincing unto
salvation. I shall reserve a fuller discussion of them
for the following chapter, which treats of this last.
But the emphatic expression THE WORLD evidently
includes all to whom the gospel under the ministration
of the Spirit comes. There is a wide-spread profession
of the truth regarding sin and righteousness and judgment. Worldly men generally acknowledge that unbelief is wrong, that Christ alone is perfect, and that
good will eventually triumph over evil. It is no deep
conviction. It does not actuate their life. But there
it lies on the surface of their minds, and they join
without compunction in the creeds or confessions of the
true Church of Christ.

(3) *It is the Holy Ghost who invites men to take
the water of life.* " The Spirit and the Bride say,
Come; and let him that heareth say, Come; and let
him that is athirst come; and whosoever will let him
take the water of life freely." This invitation of the Rev. xxii. 17

Spirit often powerfully moves those who are of the world. For the simple gospel so exactly suits the needs of man that it not seldom arrests and attracts those who do not close with its offers. It moves them in a way nothing else does. Other appeals may be of far higher intellectual fascination. But this draws the heart. It is the Spirit of God brooding on the spirit of man.

(4) *It is the Holy Ghost who warns and awakens fear.* How many of the messages to the seven Rev. ii. & iii. churches in Asia Minor are messages of alarm: they all bear his seal, " He that hath an ear, let him hear what THE SPIRIT SAITH unto the churches." He prompts the words of wisdom, which contain the offer of his grace ; and, if this offer be refused, he lifts the veil which hides that day of coming wrath, when it will be too late to cry for mercy and too late to knock Prov. i. 22— for admission.
32 ; 2 Cor.
v. 10, 11. (5) *It is the Holy Ghost who wounds the heart by his word.* These wounds, which he in faithfulness and love inflicts, are often so deep that the inmost feelings are lacerated and laid open. We see what the sword of the Spirit can do by the apostle's words to Heb. iv. 12, the Hebrew Christians. And we know what its effect
13. was in the lips of Peter and the rest when brought before the council : the high priest and they that were with him " were cut to the heart, and took counsel to Acts v. 33. slay them." So unsparingly does it discern the thoughts and intents of the heart.

(6) *And lastly, under the pressure of the striving of the Holy Ghost men may effect a great outward reformation.* They may leave off many open sins. They may take up many neglected duties. They may be conscious of strong religious impressions. They may have a temporary faith, and be sensible of an un-

wonted joy. They may take delight in approaching to
God. They may make considerable sacrifices for religion. They may engage actively in Christ's work,
and speak to others about their souls. And yet, notwithstanding all this, they may stop short of entire
self-surrender to the call and claims of the Holy Spirit.

Now we must not for a moment disparage this, which
may be called the preliminary work of the Divine
Spirit. Nay, so far from disparaging it, we have every
reason to believe that these his gracious operations in
enlightening the understanding, in convincing the
judgment, in inviting sinners to the Saviour, in warning them of their danger, in wounding the heart, and
even in persuading men to break off old habits and
begin new, in an ordinary way precede or accompany
his saving conversion of the soul to God. But if the
change wrought stops short of entire self-surrender to
God and of vital union with Jesus Christ, there is a
point, unknown to others, at which those who are thus
moved and drawn refuse to yield to the striving Spirit,
and resist him, when he urges them by every plea that
can move a reasonable being to lay hold on eternal life.

It is most affecting to trace in Scripture the examples
of those in whom the Spirit wrought some measure of
conviction, fear, submission, reformation, and obedience,
but whose goodness proved as a morning cloud and as
the early dew.

Lot's wife, under the pressure of an angel's hand,
began to flee from Sodom; but she looked back from
behind him, and became a monument of warning. Gen. xix. 16, 26.

Pharaoh, under the repeated strokes of Divine judgment, was once brought to confess, "I have sinned
. . . the Lord is righteous, and I and my people are
wicked;" yet he hardened his heart, and perished in the Exod. ix 27.
Red Sea.

Israel came out of Egypt; but with many of them God was not well pleased, and their carcases fell in the wilderness.

Heb. iii. 15—19.

On Balaam the Spirit of God came, and he prophesied of Christ, as the Star that should come out of Jacob, and with apparently deep emotion he prayed, Let me die the death of the righteous; yet he fell fighting amongst the enemies of the people of God.

Num. xxiii. 10; xxiv. 2, 17; xxxi. 8.

Orpah was so moved with affection for Naomi that she, like Ruth, went on the way with her mother-in-law to return to the land of Judah; yet at last she went back to her own people and to her gods.

Ruth i. 7, 15.

Saul, the son of Kish, as to all intellectual endowments, and administrative powers, and military prowess, and even prophetical illumination, after the Spirit of the Lord came upon him, was turned into another man; God, we read, gave him another heart: yet he did such despite to the Spirit of grace that he was forsaken of God, and died by his own hand on the mountains of Gilboa.

1 Sam. xv. 6, 9; xxviii. 6; xxxi. 4.

Ahab outwardly humbled himself, and put away many of his idolatries, yet he died impenitent.

1 Kings xxi. 27; xxii. 35.

Herod, when he heard John Baptist, did many things and heard him gladly; yet he murdered that faithful witness, and with his men of war mocked the Saviour of the world.

Mark vi. 20; Luke xxiii. 11.

The young ruler came running to Christ full of ardour, and propounded the most important question which can engage the thoughts of man: he was not far from the kingdom; but he was not prepared to give up all and follow Jesus, and went away grieved, for he had great possessions.

Mark x. 17—22.

The Scribes and Pharisees sat in Moses' seat, and taught the law, and compassed sea and land to make one proselyte; yet they rejected the counsel of God against themselves.

Matt. xxiii. 2, 15; Luke vii. 30.

Caiaphas unconsciously prophesied of the atoning work of Christ; yet himself conspired with the other priests to put him to death.

John xi. 49—53.

Judas preached the gospel of the kingdom, and wrought miracles in Christ's name, and was of the inner circle of his disciples, yet he betrayed his Lord, and perished in his iniquity.

Acts i. 25.

Ananias and *Sapphira* would give part of the price of their land; yet they lied to the Holy Ghost and died before the Lord.

ch. v.1—11

Felix trembled, while Paul reasoned of righteousness, temperance, and judgment to come, yet he put off repentance to a convenient season which never came.

ch. xxiv. 25.

Agrippa was almost persuaded to be a Christian, but he never laid hold on Christ.

ch. xxvi. 28.

Demas laboured with the chiefest of the apostles, yet after all he forsook him, having loved this present world.

Philemon 24; 2 Tim. iv. 10.

Wherein was it that these, who went so far, failed at last? With some there was a bosom sin they would not surrender, with others a craving for the world they would not overcome, with others a deadly indecision they would not put away. Lot's wife hankered after the treasures of Sodom. Pride ruined Pharaoh. Israel lusted after the good things of Egypt, and mistrusted God's promise to bring them into Canaan. Balaam loved the wages of unrighteousness. Orpah clave in heart to the gods of her country. Saul fretted against the commandment of God, and suffered the demon of jealousy to usurp the throne of his heart. Ahab weakly yielded to the wicked Jezebel. Herod submitted to the fascinations of Herodias. The young ruler trusted in riches. The Scribes and Pharisees were hypocrites. Caiaphas was blinded by bigotry. Judas loved filthy lucre. Ananias and his wife would stand well with the Church, and gain a reputation for a disinterestedness which was not theirs. Felix procrastinated. Agrippa hesitated. Demas preferred time to eternity. But so it came to pass, from one disastrous reason or another, these whose names thus stand out on the page of Scripture resisted and repulsed the Holy Spirit, when he pleaded for the heart, the whole heart, and for the life, the whole life, as a freewill offering to God.

Nor must we suppose that these signal examples represent instances which very rarely occur in the history of the Church of God. So far from this, the Bible everywhere testifies that it is no unfrequent case for men in trouble and necessity to " return and inquire early after God, to remember that God is their rock and the high God their Redeemer, and yet for their heart not to be right with him." Many of our Lord's own disciples went back and walked no more with him. No warnings against final and fatal apostasy can be more urgent than those, which St. Paul presses home on the Hebrew Christians. Yet St. Peter's words are equally solemn and severe. And St. John testifies against those who were led astray by the antichrists of his time, " They went out from us because they were not of us; for if they had been of us, they would no doubt have continued with us; but they went out that they might be made manifest that they were not all of us." Perhaps there are very few nominal Christians, who have not at different times of their life been deeply impressed. A dangerous illness, a perilous storm, a prevalent pestilence, death in the family circle, the sudden fall of a companion, or the conversion of an intimate friend, or some Scripture truth

Psa. lxxviii. 34—37.

John vi 66.

Heb. vi. 4—9; x. 26—31.

2 Pet. ii. 18—22.

1 John ii. 19.

flashing on the conscience; these or like events have led to serious thought, and crying to God, and a temporary reform of conduct. The Holy Spirit has striven with them, perhaps often, perhaps *almost* successfully. But where are they now?

The Divine Spirit, almighty though he is, does not force the citadel of man's heart. As the Father calls, but does not compel; as the Son expostulates with those who reject him, How often would I (ἠθέλησα) have gathered thy children together, as a hen gathereth her children together under her wings, and ye would not (οὐκ ἠθελήσατε); so the Holy Ghost ^{Matt. xxiii. 37.} invites, implores, and argues, and yet suffers himself to be repulsed by those of whom he testifies, "They made their hearts as an adamant stone, lest they should hear the law, and the words which the Lord of hosts hath sent IN HIS SPIRIT by the former prophets: therefore came a great wrath from the Lord of hosts." ^{Zech. vii. 12.} This is that awful obduracy of heart, of which St. Paul warned the Jews at Rome, "Well spake the Holy Ghost by Esaias the prophet unto the fathers, saying, Go unto this people, and say, Hearing ye shall hear and shall not understand; and seeing ye shall see and shall not perceive: for the heart of this people is waxed gross, and their ears are dull of hearing, and their eyes they have closed; lest they should see with their eyes, and hear with their ears, and understand with their heart, and should be converted, and I should heal them." ^{Acts xxviii. 25—27.}

And then ordinarily the strivings of the Spirit do not cease all at once, but they grow fainter and feebler. He is *grieved.* He is *vexed;* as it is written of Israel, ^{Eph. iv. 30} They rebelled and vexed (עִצְּבוּ)* his Holy Spirit: there-

---

* See note, ch. ii., p. 43.

Isa. lxiii. 10. fore he was turned to be their enemy. In some cases of open apostasy from the faith and of persevering wilful sin against light and knowledge, he is *insulted :* for the apostle asks of those who go on sinning wilfully after they have received the knowledge of the truth, " Of how much sorer punishment, suppose ye, shall he be thought worthy who hath trodden under foot the Son of God, and hath counted the blood of the covenant wherewith he was sanctified an unholy thing, and hath

Heb. x. 29 done despite unto (ἐνυβρίσας) the Spirit of grace ?" And lastly, in some awful instances of daring impiety, the Holy Spirit is *blasphemed*. This it is ·of which our Lord says, " All manner of sin and blasphemy shall be forgiven unto men, but the blasphemy of the Spirit (ἡ τοῦ Πνεύματος βλασφημία) shall not be forgiven unto men. And whosoever speaketh a word against the Son of man, it shall be forgiven him ; but whosoever speaketh against the Holy Ghost, it shall not be forgiven him, neither in this world, neither in

Matt. xii. 31, the world to come."
32.

What is the first reference in this most solemn warning of our Lord, St. Mark places beyond doubt. He uttered these words, we read, *Because they said, He*

Mark iii. 30. *hath an unclean spirit*. In that gospel also the expression, " blasphemy of the Spirit," is explained more fully as " blasphemy against (εἰς) the Holy Ghost :" and for the words " neither in this world, neither in the world to come," is substituted their plain meaning, " hath never forgiveness, but is in danger of (ἔνοχος, *obnoxious*, cf. Heb. ii. 15, where it is rendered *subject to*, and 1 Cor. xi. 27, guilty) eternal damnation." The phrase imports, according to Hebrew usage, " shall NEVER be forgiven." But although this warning first referred to the blasphemous charge of the Pharisees, it is a voice for all ages, and should guard us against

CHAP. VI.

admitting for a moment the suspicion that there can be any compact between Christ and Belial; against 2 Cor. vi. 15. perverting the minds of those inquiring the way of life; against attributing to evil motives in others that Matt. xii 23 which may in truth be the prompting of the Holy 24. Ghost, and above all, against any presumptuous defamation of the Person or personal work of the same Eternal Spirit. These are perils against which we are here more obviously warned. But there is, without doubt designedly, an obscurity hanging over this sin against the Holy Ghost—a merciful obscurity warning us against approaching near the confines of a sin for which there is no forgiveness. It is the danger signal. It is the alarm bell. It is the voice, " Keep thy foot." It is the cry, " Flee from the wrath to come."

How far this unpardonable sin against the Holy Ghost is to be identified with " the sin unto death," of which St. John speaks, is a question which can never 1 John v. 16, be absolutely determined by man. From the context 17. in the epistle we should gather that open, deliberate, persistent denial of Christ by one, who was once a professed believer, is the sin unto death. For death in the 16th verse is evidently contrasted with the spiritual and eternal life spoken of; and though we are imme- ver. 11, 12. diately afterward assured that no one really born of ver. 18. God sins unto death, yet the sinner here condemned is professedly a brother. For all other sins the children of God are encouraged hopefully and confidently to pray; but such an apostate puts himself beyond the pale of their prayers. Such an one must be cast out of the church, and left in the hands of God. There are thus solemn features of resemblance and points of contact betwixt the sin against the Holy Ghost and the sin unto death. And farther, we should gather both from our Lord's words and from those of his apostle that there was only one kind of sin which could not be forgiven. But, as before, an obscurity veils the exact nature of a sin, from which it is our duty to pray that we may be kept at the greatest possible distance.

And although the cases may be very few in which sin reaches such a climax of blasphemy and apostasy, nevertheless if it be true that the Holy Spirit thus strives with many whom he never savingly quickens unto life eternal, if he enlightens their understanding, and convicts them of sin, righteousness, and judgment, if he invites them to partake of Christ, and warns them with alarming expostulations of the peril of rejecting him, if he cuts deep into their heart by the two-edged sword of his truth, and even persuades them to a vast outward reformation—if notwithstanding all this he may be resisted, repulsed, and finally driven away by some secretly cherished lust, or invincible worldliness, or deadly indecision, surely the voice is loud indeed to those who are lingering on the threshold of the kingdom, To-day, while it is called to-day, harden not your hearts, as in the provocation in the day of temptation in the wilderness, lest haply of them, as of Israel of old, God swear in his wrath, They shall not enter into my rest. The habit of vacillation, of halting between two opinions, of oscillation between the world and Christ, in itself a most unnatural and irksome state, may yet by long indulgence become a second nature. There are those who open the Scriptures, and who regularly go to the house of prayer, and listen to the everlasting gospel, expecting, whenever they do this, to be somewhat moved, and indeed disappointed if they are not conscious of some emotion, but yet who refuse to surrender their heart to God. They are ever learning, but never able to come to the knowledge of the truth. Let such beware. They are striving against One who will not always strive with them. They are resisting the Eternal Spirit, of whose words none are more solemn, none are more frequently exemplified than these, To-day is the day of salvation; ye know not what shall be upon the morrow.

2 Tim. iii. 7.

CHAPTER VII

THE HOLY SPIRIT QUICKENING THE SOUL TO LIFE

THERE are few scenes of interest even in the Gospel narratives to compare with the nightly interview between our Lord and Nicodemus.* That anxious inquirer was of exalted position—a ruler of the Jews; of high repute for sanctity—one of the select and exclusive caste, a Pharisee; of eminent learning—a distinguished master (ὁ διδάσκαλος, the article has at least this force) in Israel. Yet within there was that secret dissatisfaction of which he was probably half-unconscious, but which ever lurks in a heart that is not at peace with God. But a teacher came to Jerusalem; his mission was attested by undeniable and holy miracles; and he came proclaiming glad tidings of peace. This fact fastened on the unsuspected or stifled disquietude of Nicodemus. Peace—this was what he wanted and had not. His fasts, prayers, alms—if he recalled them to mind—sufficed not to allay the craving within. Outwardly he may have preserved the dignity of his demeanour; but at night, through the dark unlighted streets, he wends his way to the obscure lodging which shelters the Prophet of Nazareth. The garb of Jesus would mark him as belonging to the poor of this world. A day spent, as his days ever were,

---

* See note, *Preface*, page ii.

in works of mercy, would have left him weary at night-
fall. The sorrow of sojourning in a world of sin had
doubtless already left its deep traces on his brow. Yet see John viii. 57.
we may well believe what goodness and love beamed
in his countenance as he argued with Nicodemus,
calmly, for he knew his own strength—earnestly, for
he knew the preciousness of the issue at stake. This
secret conversation we are permitted to share. We
need not with some suppose that John overheard it, or
that Christ afterwards related it. It is enough that
the Holy Spirit, who often moved the sacred writers to
record what no human eye witnessed and no ear heard,
inspired the evangelist to relate this for the highest
good of his church.

In his opening words, *Rabbi, we know that thou art
a teacher come from God,* etc., Nicodemus recognises
Jesus Christ as sent from God, but only as a human
teacher accredited by divine miracles. In his reply,
our Lord passes by the legal righteousness of Nicodemus, his knowledge of the law, his dignity in the
Jewish church, and even the admission which he had
now made, and comes at once to that which is absolutely essential—the new birth of the soul to God.
Except a man be born again (ἄνωθεν, or " from
above," a word seems designedly chosen which embraces both thoughts), *he cannot see the kingdom of
God,* including in this the kingdom of grace here with
all its mysteries, and the kingdom of glory hereafter
with all its manifested splendours. The expression of
amazement, *How can a man be born when he is old ?*
(γέρων ὤν, not only *adult,* but *aged*) proves that Nicodemus felt these words were meant for himself—an
old man. The Jews were wont to speak of a proselyte when baptized as *a child new born ;* but the
general declaration " Except a man be born again," etc.,

which would include Jews as well as Gentiles, the legally righteous as well as publicans and sinners, seems to have banished every such usual metaphor from the mind of Nicodemus, and to have awakened, not contemptuous, but unfeigned astonishment.

Christ does not soften aught. We might anticipate new marvels of grace from the repetition of the *Verily, verily, I say unto thee;* and he reveals the agent of this new and heavenly birth, even the Holy Ghost. *Except a man be born of water and of the Spirit, he cannot enter into the kingdom of God* The Jews were accustomed to receive proselytes by baptism.

John i. 26. John came saying, "I baptize with water." Jesus was now by the hands of his disciples beginning to ch. iii. 22; iv. baptize large numbers. But the Pharisees and 1, 2. lawyers, many of them, rejected the counsel of God Luke vii. 29. against themselves, being not baptized of John. Hence *born of water*, Nicodemus might understand as requisite for neophytes and repenting sinners. But here was the inexplicable mystery to him, who was then only groping after the light, in the closing words, born of water AND OF THE SPIRIT. They are equivalent to "born not of water only, but of water and of the Spirit." And this Jesus declared to be essential for entrance into the kingdom of God—the baptism of water, as his appointed ordinance for admission into the visible church being " *generally* necessary for salvation" by reason of obedience to his command; the baptism of the Spirit, that inward and spiritual grace, of which water is the outward and visible sign, being *absolutely* essential by reason of the heavenly nature of that kingdom into which nothing unregenerate can enter. The same distinction is observed by our Lord in his evangelistic charge, when he says, "Go ye into all the world, and preach the Gospel to every

CHAP. VII.

creature: he that believeth and is baptized shall be saved; but he that believeth not shall be damned." For baptism is to the new birth what confession is to faith: and while " With the heart man believeth unto righteousness, with the mouth confession is made unto salvation."

Mark xvi. 15 16

Rom. x. 10.

Our Lord proceeds further to explain and enforce the spiritual birth, contrasting it with the natural birth. The flesh, *i.e.*, fallen human nature, can only produce flesh; therefore, could a man enter the second time into his mother's womb and be born, this heavenly regeneration would not be effected thereby. It must be a power from without acting upon and working in man, even the power of the Holy Ghost. The words stand forth as written with a sunbeam. *Ye* (ὑμεῖς, all the children of Adam except the Son of Man) *must be born again.* And this birth of the Spirit is further set forth in pictorial language* derived from the wind and its mysterious changes.

---

* There is much controversy whether the word translated *wind* were not better rendered *spirit*, and the whole verse applied to the Divine Spirit, and with reason, for (1) it is the same word, πνεῦμα, in the Greek throughout; (2) this is the only passage in the New Testament, though the word occurs about three hundred and seventy times, in which it is translated *wind*; (3) there are other words for *wind* in the New Testament, as ἄνεμος, πνοή, and, if the distinction were intended to be drawn, this would seem the place for the choice of one of these words, even as in the description of the descent of the Holy Ghost on Pentecost, where the simile of the mighty rushing wind is expressed by one word (πνοή), and the Spirit by another (πνεῦμα); (4) the difficulty is great in speaking of *the will* of the wind, " the wind bloweth *where it listeth* (ὅπου θέλει)," but the expression, " The Spirit breatheth where He wills," exactly answers to St. Paul's words; (5) the words rendered *the sound thereof* (τὴν φωνὴν αὐτοῦ) would be more naturally translated *his voice*—compare ch. v. 37, and consider the greatly preponderating use of the word, φωνή, in the New Testament, for sound

1 Cor. xii. 11.

Nicodemus still asks *How?* which is so often the difficulty with those who demand to know every step of the process in Divine operations. But the Lord replies, Art thou a master (ὁ διδάσκαλος, "the teacher" of others, yea of Israel), and knowest not these things? This proves that the new birth of the soul to God was one even of the elementary truths of the Old Covenant; and so we find circumcision of the heart, the creation of a new heart and new spirit, the taking away of the stony heart, and the indwelling of the Holy Ghost, insisted upon both in the law and in the prophets.

Deut. x. 16; xxx. 6; Isa. lxlii. 11; Ezek. xviii. 31; xxxvi. 26.

Furthermore, Christ adds, "If I have told you earthly things and ye believe not, how shall ye believe if I tell you of heavenly things?" By "earthly things" he signifies this new birth of the soul which

---

accompanied with articulate speech; (6) the words *cometh* and *goeth* are more naturally used of a person than of *wind*, which would rather be said to rise or to cease; (7) the comparison, if *wind* is retained, would seem rather to require that the last clause should run, "So doth the Spirit work on every new-born soul." These reasons seem sufficient for our interpreting this verse with Origen, Augustine, Bengel, etc., entirely of the Holy Ghost. As when we read, "The light shineth in darkness, and the darkness comprehendeth it not," we understand not created light, but Christ, the Increate Light, though the truth is couched in pictorial language,—so here, when we read, "The Spirit bloweth (or "breatheth," πνεῖ) where he wills, and thou knowest his voice, but canst not tell whence he cometh or whither he goeth," we understand not created breath but the Increate Spirit, though the truth is couched in pictorial language, derived from the wind and its mysterious changes. And now the last clause—*So is every one that is born of the Spirit*—will appropriately signify, as the Holy Spirit is free and sovereign in his operations, so every one that is born of God is set free. The bonds of sin are broken; and even as the new-born child emerges from the darkness and constraint of the womb into the light of life, so the new-born soul, being emancipated from the thraldom of sin, comes into the liberty of the Gospel, and enjoys the freedom of that kingdom which owns no slaves.

ch. i. 5.

must take place on earth; for " to the heavenly apprehension of Jesus Christ those things are earthly which
are transacted on the earth, though to us who dwell
in the dust they appear most heavenly : regeneration
comes from heaven, but is not wrought in heaven"
(Bengel). What the heavenly things themselves are,
Christ rather hints at than reveals to Nicodemus. Yet
he here opens the chart of salvation : he points to the
path of life : and clearer glimpses into the glory beyond
are vouchsafed during the course of his ministry, and John xiv. 2;
a fuller apocalypse to the beloved disciple in Patmos.   xvii. 5, 24 ;
xx. 17.

But having declared the absolute necessity of the
new birth, and its author, even the Holy Ghost, the
Lord proceeds to set forth his own atoning sacrifice,
by which truth the Spirit quickens man to life ; for the
soul is born again by the incorruptible seed of the
word, even the word of the Gospel. And by the mar- 1 Pet. i. 23—
vellous type of the brazen serpent he prefaces the   25.
fullest, freest, richest proclamation of evangel love in
those unfathomable words, "God so loved the world
that he gave his only begotten Son, that whosoever believeth on him should not perish but have everlasting
life."

I have dwelt the longer on this conversation of our
Lord with Nicodemus, for nowhere else is this fundamental truth more plainly and unhesitatingly affirmed ;
viz., that he who would enter the kingdom of God
must needs be born again of the Holy Spirit. The
subject is full of solemn awe. Life is in itself a
mystery. God is its author and giver. Even of the
vegetable and animal creations we read, "Thou sendest
forth thy Spirit, and they are created, and thou renewest
the face of the earth." We have no reason to believe Psa. civ. 30
that the highest archangel could make the humblest
herb yielding seed and fruit after its kind, or animate

the meanest worm that crawls upon the ground. So far as we know, God has kept life in his own hands. And if it be so with regard to the lowest types of organic and animated nature, the initial life in man's own spirit, the life to Godward, may well be of all subjective mysteries the subtlest and the most profound. Yet is it so absolutely essential, that without it we are assured no one can even see the kingdom of God. May those who read these pages lift up their heart in prayer, that the same Divine Spirit may lead us by the hand every step of this momentous investigation.

It will prove of some assistance to remind ourselves of the other names, by which this vital change within is designated in Holy Scripture.

The expressions "born again" or "born of the Spirit," which our Lord employed when conversing with Nicodemus, are evidently equivalent to "born of God." The first passage, referred to in the margin, is the fullest; for there we learn "the sons of God were born, not of blood, nor of the will of the flesh, nor of the will of man, but of God."

John i. 13; 1 John iii. 9; iv. 7; v. 1, 4, 18.

Again, this new birth is called "being quickened" or "quickened together with Christ," which work of grace is ascribed to the richness of God's sovereign mercy when we were dead in trespasses and sins. It is afterwards in that epistle described by three figures in one verse, as awaking from sleep, arising from death, and being illuminated by Christ's light. "Awake thou that sleepest, and arise from the dead, and Christ shall give thee light" ($\epsilon\pi\iota\phi\alpha\upsilon\sigma\epsilon\iota$ $\sigma o\iota$).

Ephes. ii. 1 —5.

ch. v. 14.

It is sometimes, as stated above, called in the Old Testament "circumcision of the heart;" and sometimes "the creation of a new heart and a new spirit;" or "the taking away of the stony heart and the imparting of a heart of flesh."

It is also called "conversion." "Sinners shall be converted unto thee." "Lest they should understand and convert and be healed." "Repent ye, therefore, and be converted." "He that converteth a sinner from the error of his way," etc. The substantive occurs but once, " declaring the conversion (τὴν ἐπιστροφήν) of the Gentiles." The word signifies the turning of the whole man from sin to holiness, and from Satan to God.

Psa. li. 3.

Isa. vi. 10, quoted Matt. xiii. 15; Mark iv. 12; John xii. 40; Acts xxviii. 27. Acts iii. 19. James v. 20. Acts xv. 3.

Again, it is often called "repentance" (μετάνοια, "change of mind"), and often "faith," though when repentance only is named it includes faith, and where faith only is named it includes repentance. Both are expressed in that which St. Paul declared to be the substance of his testimony, "repentance toward God and faith toward our Lord Jesus Christ." More than once it is called "reconciliation with God."

ch. xx. 21.

Rom. v. 10; 2 Cor. v. 20.

Again, it is described as " receiving Christ," and so " becoming sons of God." This receiving Christ is the same as believing the record God has given of his Son; and this leads us back to an expression quoted shortly before, " Being born again, not of corruptible seed, but of incorruptible, by the word of God, which liveth and abideth for ever." The word of the gospel is the instrument of the new birth.

John i. 12.

1 John v. 9, 10.

1 Pet. i. 23.

Yet again, it is spoken of, as " coming out of darkness into the marvellous light of God," as " those who were darkness becoming light in the Lord," and—a yet stronger image—as " a passing out of death into life."

ch. ii. 9.

Ephes. v. 8.

John v. 24.

Once the change is described as " living no more for ourselves but for him who died for us "—a new principle of life actuating the believer—so that the apostle affirms, " If any man be in Christ he is a new creation (καινὴ κτίσις); old things have passed away—behold all things have become new."

2 Cor. v. 17.

And—to quote but one passage more—St. Paul

Tit. iii. 5.

writes to Titus that "God saved us according to his mercy by the washing of regeneration and the renewing of the Holy Ghost."

Here we have at least twenty different expressions— *born again, born of the Spirit, born of God, born of the incorruptible seed of the word, being quickened, arising from the dead, conversion, circumcision of the heart, the creation of a new heart and new spirit, the heart of stone becoming the heart of flesh, repentance, faith, reconciliation with God, receiving Christ, believing God's record to his Son, awaking from sleep, coming out of darkness into light, darkness becoming light, passing from death to life, a new creation, salvation by the washing of regeneration and by the renewing of the Holy Ghost*—expressions, in which many and various figures are employed, but all indicating how great and radical the change is. This is the new birth of the soul to God by the operation of the Holy Ghost.

Now in this new birth the Spirit's preparative work is, to a great extent, the same in those who by the grace of God yield to his Divine striving, and in those who resist it and perish. See this proved from Scripture in the last chapter. But in all those who are truly born of God, his gracious work is effectual and fruitful and permanent.

The Holy Spirit enlightens their understanding, so that "the light of the glorious gospel of Christ, who is the image of God, shines upon them"—yea, into them —for "God, who commanded the light to shine out of darkness, shines in our hearts to give the light of the knowledge of the glory of God in the face of Jesus Christ." The eye of the soul is opened. They who were blind see. They see Christ.

2 Cor. iv. 4 —6.

The Holy Spirit convinces them of sin, of righteousness, and of judgment. Upon this our Lord's words are express: "If I depart I will send the Comforter unto you: and when he is come he will reprove* (ἐλέγξει) the world of sin, and of righteousness, and of judgment; of sin, because they believe not on me; of righteousness, because I go to my Father and ye see me no more; of judgment, because the prince of this world is judged." John xvi. 7 —11.

Let us look into these "few deep and wonderful words" more closely.†

The Comforter shall convince the world of (περί, " concerning ") *sin, and of* (περί) *righteousness, and of* (περί) *judgment*—i. e., what sin really is, what righteousness is, what judgment is; what is the true nature of each; of what each essentially consists.

The world has no real sense of what SIN is. Some sinful acts worldly men will acknowledge to be wrong, but that from which these acts flow—a heart by nature alien from God, and by practice refusing God's reconciling grace in Christ, that unbelief which is *the root-sin* of all others—they esteem of little or no moment; it does not enter into their estimate of character, their own, or others. Now the Comforter convinces men of this sin, either for their salvation during their day of grace, or, if they persevere to the end in refusing all the offers of Divine love, for their eternal condemnation. Of this the Jews in that age were the most signal example: as a nation they refused and crucified the Lord of glory; the Holy Spirit came down from heaven; some were brought to true repentance, others hardened their hearts to their own ruin.

---

* "It is difficult to give in one word the deep meaning of that translated 'reprove:' 'convince' approaches, perhaps, the nearest to it, but does not express the double sense which is manifestly here intended of a *convincing* unto salvation, and a *convicting* unto condemnation."—*Alford.*

† See note, *Preface*, page ii.

The world, which knows not what sin really is, knows not what true righteousness is. Men imagine an external morality will suffice, and desire not the righteousness of God. Hence, when the perfectly Righteous One came to his own, his own received him not: they condemned the Holy One of God as a malefactor; but he, rejected of men, ascended to the Father, and there presented his own spotless obedience to the scrutiny of infinite justice and infinite love. The world saw him no more; but the Great Surety having paid man's debt on the cross, appears in heaven for man, our sinless advocate and mediator, the man Christ Jesus. His mission of the Comforter proved the acceptance of his mighty work. This likewise resulted in the saving conviction of some, the condemning conviction of others. Thus, as the Divine Spirit in convincing of sin does not stop short at any sinful acts, but goes down to and exposes the very germ and source of sin, which is unbelief, so in convincing of righteousness he does not stop short at any works of the law, which can never justify the sinner before God, but rises up to and exhibits the only justifying righteousness, even that which is of God by faith, and which is the only spring of acceptable and evangelical holiness.

There remains one more great conviction needful for man, the conviction of judgment. Sin and righteousness are directly opposed one to another. Unbelief and faith are the fruitful principles of all the evil and of all the good manifest in the intelligent creation. The most casual glance upon this our fallen world reveals the awful strife in which these two are engaged. The conflict and collision are tremendous, now one apparently succeeding, now another. But no casual glance can reveal what shall be the issue of their strife. No eye can discern it that is not opened by the Holy Spirit.

Even now, when the gospel has been militant for eighteen hundred years, only one fourth of the world is even *professedly* Christian. Even now to the eye of sense the conflict might seem interminable ; and if it be so now, how much more when these words were uttered, *The Comforter will convince the world of judgment, because the prince of this world* (*i.e.*, the devil, see ch. xii. 31, xiv. 30, etc.) *hath been judged* (κέκριται). O glorious conviction! Here is the issue of the conflict. The wicked one, who is the tempter to all evil and the accuser of the brethren, is himself accused, condemned, sentenced, and to the eye of him who sees the end from the beginning cast out into the abyss of wrath. Behold the victory of faith in him who is the Author and Finisher of the faith! He was in an upper chamber in Jerusalem pouring consolation into the hearts of eleven sorrowing disciples ; but his eye ranges from the creation to the final judgment, and, himself about to die, he declares his great foe and ours to be for ever judged and overcome. Of this judgment the Comforter convinces the world ; those who are saved, during their day of grace ; those who perish, in eternity, when the overthrow of the enemies of Christ is no longer a matter of faith but of manifestation.

Our digression on these words has been somewhat extended, but their exceeding importance claimed it. To resume—when the Holy Spirit savingly convinces of sin, righteousness, and judgment, *the soul is brought to self-despair and self-surrender.* Such was the issue of his gracious work on the day of Pentecost, " They were pricked in their heart, and said unto Peter and to the rest of the apostles, Men and brethren, what shall we do ?" It was the same in the conversion of Saul of Tar- Acts ii. 37. sus, " He, trembling and astonished, said, Lord, what wilt thou have me to do ?" It was the same with the jailer, ch. ix. 6.

"Trembling, he fell down before Paul and Silas . . .
and said, Sirs, what must I do to be saved?" The re-
bellion of man's heart is broken down. Pride is crushed.
Human reliances are seen to fail. And the will of the
convicted sinner submits to the mightier will of God.

Acts xvi. 29, 30.

This self-surrender leads to *prayer*. The Holy Spirit
is a Spirit of grace and of supplications. So at Pentecost prayer was the first duty urged by St. Peter when
he reminded them of the words of the prophet, ". Whosoever shall call upon the name of the Lord shall be
saved." We are not told what those supplications
were; but doubtless they were very urgent and wrestling and prevalent that day—heaven's gate was be-
sieged with the prayers of three thousand stricken
consciences. So with the apostle of the Gentiles, this
was the first sign of life named by the Lord to Ananias
—"Behold he prayeth"—and this was the cry of the
soul to God-ward on which Ananias laid such stress.
"And now, why tarriest thou? arise and be baptized
and wash away thy sins, having called (ἐπικαλεσάμενος)
on the name of the Lord." We know not, but we may
in part surmise what were the confessions and cries for
mercy that rose from the bruised and contrite heart of
a Paul. Such was the prayer of the publican when
standing afar off he would not lift up so much as his
eyes unto heaven, but smote upon his breast, saying,
"God be merciful (ἱλάσθητι)—" be propitiated") to me
the sinner."

Zech. xii. 10

Acts ii. 21.

ch. ix. 11; xxii. 16.

Luke xviii. 13.

And in closest connexion with this is *the obedience of
faith*. The gospel, we read, is made known to all
nations for the obedience of faith. And St. Peter
writes, "Ye have purified your souls in obeying the
truth through the Spirit." The command is, "Look
unto me and be ye saved;" and this mighty act is described by the prophet, "I will pour upon the house of

Rom. xvi. 26.

1 Pet. i. 22.

Isa. xlv. 22.

David and upon the inhabitants of Jerusalem the Spirit of grace and of supplications; and they shall look upon Me whom they have pierced, and mourn for him as one mourneth for his only son, and shall be in bitterness for him as one that is in bitterness for his first-born." Zech. xii. 10. That Jesus Christ, pierced on the cross, is the One to whom this obedient look of faith is directed, we are assured. The obedience, we observe, is rendered not John xix. 34, without but in the power of the Holy Spirit. Faith is 37. the free gift of God. And so the apostle writes to the Corinthians : " Ye are justified in the name of the Lord Jesus (here is the ground of salvation), and by the Spirit of our God " (here is the power in which we embrace it). This is that look of the soul towards Christ, which corresponds to the look of the dying Israelites upon the brazen serpent. Every one that looks lives. O what an unspeakably blessed moment Numb. xxi. for the soul is that, when, every other hope being re- 8, 9; John nounced, the sinner resigns himself to Jesus Christ! iii. 14, 15. It is the mariner, who has long lashed himself to the wrecked and sinking vessel, cutting the ropes which bind him to that fatal hull, and casting himself into the life-boat. He is saved!

But let me name two or three further stages of this new creation of the Spirit. When the sinner has thus cast himself on the Saviour, and the atoning blood of Christ is applied to the conscience by the Holy Spirit, there follows *peace with God*. Through Jesus the penitent believer has access by one Spirit unto the Father, Ephes. ii. 18. not as in after days with an experienced and proven confidence, but often with a peculiar freshness of delight.

And now first is that divinest affection, *the love of God*, felt in the soul. All the joy of human life is from human love. But he has never tasted Divine joy, who

has not tasted Divine love. Now when, being justified
by faith, we have peace with God through our Lord
Jesus Christ, "the love of God is shed abroad in our
hearts by the Holy Ghost which is given unto us."
"We love him because he first loved us." Our love is
the repercussion of the beams of his love. It may be
very faint and feeble at first, but it is true; and the
believer is henceforth enrolled among the glorious company of those who love God.

Rom. v. 5.

1 John iv. 19.

From love flows *godly sorrow for sin*. It is very
important not to confound *knowledge of sin*, which is
one of the first works of the Holy Spirit in the new
creation, with *gracious sorrow for sin*, which is one of
his later works. There are, alas! many who hold the
process of his Divine operations in the soul to be this:
firstly, penitential sorrow, secondly, faith, and lastly,
holiness. If they did not name any order at all, but
only said that godly sorrow was a needful element in all
spiritual life, it would not be so material; but by
assigning it the first place they often greatly discourage
those who are feeling after God. The anxious inquirer
comes to them and asks in deepest solicitude, "How
shall I draw near to God?" And they answer, "Be
sorry for your past sins, and carry the load of your
grief to the mercy-seat in earnest prayer." Well, the
man makes the effort; he kneels down; he confesses
his sins to God; but the confession does not affect his
heart. He rises from his knees lifeless and loveless.
Grief flows from love: we only grieve for having grieved
one we love. Nor is it enough to say, the Holy Spirit
can make such a man feel the sins he confesses by his
omnipotent grace; for to this it may be sufficiently
answered, that to feel true contrition without love is
not a natural but a spiritual impossibility, and that the
Divine Spirit, though almighty, works by his own

laws, and not in antagonism to them. You can never wring the drops of gracious grief out of servile fear. It is not there. The alarmed sinner is charged, Be sorry for your sins. And he tries, he toils, he argues, he upbraids himself, he presents his transgressions in many lights, he lacerates himself with self-reproaches; but the obstinate obdurate heart will not grieve. Grief flows from love, and he does not love God.

Nay, rather the true place of godly sorrow in the new birth of the soul is that indicated above. It does not precede, but succeed, conviction and faith and peace and love. Only let me premise two or three words by way of caution. These successive stages are by no means always to be traced by the convert in whose heart they are taking place, and far less by others. Again, sometimes one affection so predominates, as love, for instance, that the others, though really there, are concealed : nor does one affection expel another. And again sometimes the whole work is so rapid, as with the jailer at Philippi, that in a few brief hours the soul has experienced all, and can only say, "One thing I know, that whereas I was blind, now I see." It is with the new as with the natural creation ; there are great archetypes, but nothing rigidly uniform in God's works. Truth is not crystallized into one shape. Where the Spirit of the Lord is, there is liberty. And herein the illumination of the Holy Ghost may be likened to the natural light of the sun. The pure white rays of sunlight may be resolved into their component colours, in which there is a constant invariable succession—red, orange, yellow, green, blue, indigo, violet. But when the sunshine paints the clouds or the flowers, now one hue, now another prevails. For the white light of the sun is a composition of all hues, and when it falls on any object is decomposed, a part of it being absorbed by,

or transmitted through the object, and a part only
reflected, and thus the object appears to have the colour
peculiar to this latter part.* Still, though the appear-
ances are so diverse, you cannot derange the natural
order of colours in the light, though when you see them
all as refracted in the prism, one insensibly melts into
another. And so with the entrance of truth into the
soul, there is a Divine order, and it is, I believe, that
indicated above—conviction, faith, peace, love, godly
sorrow—though it may often be hard to say where one
ends and another begins.

We have a striking illustration of this in the conversion of Martin Luther. Staupitz, the vicar-general,
had said to him, "Instead of torturing yourself for your
faults, cast yourself into the arms of your Redeemer."
But Luther, says his biographer, could not find in
himself the repentance he thought necessary to his
salvation, and answered, "How can I dare believe in
the favour of God, so long as there is in me no real conversion? I must be changed before he can receive
me." Then he hears this answer from the vicar-
general—or rather, he does not believe that it comes
from a man; it seems to him a voice resounding from
heaven—"There is," said Staupitz, "no true repentance but that which begins in the love of God and of
righteousness. That which some fancy to be the end
of repentance is only its beginning. In order to be
filled with the love of that which is good, you must
first be filled with the love of God. If you wish to be
really converted, do not follow these mortifications and
penances. Love him, who has first loved you." Luther
listens, and listens again. These consolations fill him
with a joy before unknown, and impart to him new light.

---

* See Lardner's Museum, vol. vii., 66.

"It is Jesus Christ," thinks he in his heart, "who comforts me so wonderfully by these sweet and salutary words." *In order to repentance we must love God.* Guided by this new light he consulted the Scriptures. He looked to all the passages which speak of repentance and conversion; and the words so dreaded hitherto (to use his own expressions) became to him an agreeable pastime and the sweetest refreshment; they seem to run to him from all sides, to smile, to spring up, and play around him. *

To sum up the last three paragraphs,—godly sorrow flows from love. We love him who died for us. Our sins nailed him to the accursed tree. The fountain of grief is unsealed. It is a tender, deep, gracious sorrow. It is not that bitter sorrow of the world which worketh death, but that godly sorrow which worketh repentance to salvation not to be repented of. Behold the wondrous transformation! the soul loves what once it loathed, and loathes what once it loved. Once it loved sin, and was at enmity with God. Now it loves God, and dreads sin as the greatest of all evils. It is a new life. 2 Cor. vii. 10.

But man's life is not before God only; he lives a man amongst men. And this mighty inward change will have its corresponding outward manifestation. Faith in Christ will assuredly, sooner or later, be followed by *confession of Christ.* This is one great reason of the divinely appointed ordinance of baptism. Baptism is the expression of faith. So, in the instances named above, the converts in Jerusalem on the day of Pentecost, the contrite Saul at Damascus, and the believing jailer, with all his house, at Philippi, were openly sealed by baptism for the service of their Lord. And so is it now—the penitent believer, if unbaptized, will seek Acts ii. 33; ix. 18; xvi. 33.

---

* D'Aubigné, Reformation, vol. i., pp. 181, 182.

for admission by baptism into the visible Church of Christ; if baptized, will declare his adherence to the vows of his baptism by an open and credible profession, whose he is and whom he serves. The Master will not own disciples, who refuse to confess him. They may be secret inquirers after him or secret followers of him for a season; but the time will assuredly come when they will have to confess Christ, and the cause of Christ. So it was with Nicodemus and Joseph of Arimathea; the hour came which brought their hidden faith to light. And so is it with all, for Jesus says, " Whosoever shall confess me before men, him will I confess also before my Father in heaven; but whosoever shall deny me before men, him will I also deny before my Father in heaven. . . . And he that taketh not his cross and followeth me is not worthy of me." Nor is this outward confession of faith to be made independently of, but dependently on the power of the Holy Ghost. One and another openly saying, I am the Lord's, and subscribing with the hand to the Lord, follows the effusion of the Spirit. Jesus himself, when baptized, was praying. And they who are truly sealed unto the day of redemption are sealed with the Holy Spirit of promise.

Matt. x. 32, 33, 38.

Isa. xliv. 3 —5.
Luke iii. 21.

Ephes. i. 13 ; iv. 30.

And now is the soul ready for service. The Spirit of God has illuminated the understanding, has convinced the conscience, has brought the sinner to self-despair, and the rebel to self-surrender, has prompted the cry for mercy, has bidden the suppliant look on Christ and live, and has enabled the obedience of faith, has given peace with God, has awakened the first strivings of the love of God in the heart, has quickened the compunctions of godly sorrow, and has led the disciple openly to confess that Lord and Master to whom he has secretly plighted his faith. This is that which is born of the

Spirit. The man is now a spiritual man, and hence- 1 Cor. ii. 15. forth minds the things of the Spirit. This is the work- Rom. viii. 5. manship of God. And where this work has been Ephes. ii. 10. wrought we may humbly but confidently share the apostolic assurance, " He which hath begun a good work in you will perform it until the day of Jesus Christ." Phil. i. 6.

If any who read these pages have reason to fear that this mighty change, this new creation, this birth of the soul, has never taken place in them, God of his infinite mercy grant that they may lay to heart the words of our Lord to Nicodemus, from which all who touch this subject must feel its exceeding moment, " Except a man be born again, he cannot see, he cannot enter the kingdom of God." Men may enter the visible church by baptism ; they may enter the societies and the assemblies of the people of God; they may enter the circle of those who gather round the table of their Lord. But unless they are born again they cannot enter the kingdom of God. And what is exclusion from that kingdom? Let the Master answer, " There shall be weeping and gnashing of teeth when ye shall see Abraham and Isaac and Jacob and all the prophets in the kingdom of God, and you yourselves thrust out." Luke xiii 28 But—blessed assurance—to-day is the day of salvation. The fountain is flowing yet. And the great voice, with which Jesus cried aloud on the last day of the Feast of Tabernacles, yet rings in our ears, " If any man thirst, let him come to me and drink." This, we read, spake John vii. 37. he of the Spirit, which they that believe on him should receive.

CHAPTER VIII

THE HOLY SPIRIT SANCTIFYING THE BELIEVER

WE considered in the last chapter the work of the Divine Spirit in quickening the soul to life. We have now therefore to treat of a new-born soul, alive unto God, justified by faith in Jesus Christ, and animated by the breath of the Holy Ghost. Such an one is the subject of the sanctifying grace of the Holy Spirit. The morning has dawned : the light must shine more and more unto the perfect day. The seed has germinated: it must grow and spring up, and bring forth fruit, first the blade, then the ear, after that the full corn in the ear. The soul is new born; it must thrive and increase until it comes unto a perfect man, unto the measure of the stature of the fulness of Christ. The new creation is begun : the Divine counsel and operation must be carried on, until God looking upon it shall say, Behold, it is very good. This progressive work is sanctification. This sanctification is wrought by the Holy Ghost.

In a few weighty words Owen says, " Sanctification is an immediate work of the Spirit of God on the souls of believers, purifying and cleansing their natures from the pollution and uncleanness of sin, renewing in them the image of God, and thereby enabling them, from a spiritual and habitual principle of grace, to yield obedience unto God, according unto the tenor and terms of the new covenant, by virtue of the life and

Prov. iv. 18.

Mark iv. 28.

Eph. iv. 13.

death of Jesus Christ. Or, more briefly, it is the universal renovation of our natures by the Holy Spirit into the image of God through Jesus Christ. . . . This work is progressive, and admits of degrees. One may be more sanctified and more holy than another, who is yet truly sanctified and truly holy. It is begun at once, and carried on gradually."

It is most necessary for us to hold this truth firmly and intelligently in these dangerous times, when many fix their thoughts so exclusively on the new birth that they practically slight the need of growth in the Divine life ; and others presume to affirm that those who are in Christ are not only perfectly justified, which is true, but also perfectly sanctified, which is untrue.

Here it were enough to quote the emphatic words of St. Peter. "Beloved, beware lest ye fall from your own steadfastness : but GROW (αὐξάνετε, or "increase") IN GRACE and in the knowledge of our Lord and Saviour Jesus Christ." To which precept the brief but exhaustless promise of St. James corresponds, "He giveth more grace." 2 Pet. iii. 18.

James iv. 6.

The contrast between a living and a dead soul is infinite ; but then the contrast between two living souls may be vast indeed. We see this in lower regions than Divine things. Take physical powers : you cannot compare a lifeless corpse and a living man—the case does not admit of degrees ; but see two men, one vigorous, strong, robust, active,—the other, weak, suffering, apathetic, helpless ; both alive, but what different degrees of life ! Take property : you cannot compare solvency and criminal bankruptcy—the case does not admit of degrees ; but see two men, one barely able to keep body and soul together,—the other, with ample means for himself and others ; both free from debt, but what different degrees of substance ! Take

mental talents : you cannot compare sanity and idiotcy—
the case does not admit of degrees ; but see two men,
one his mind scarcely raised above the ground on which
he treads,—the other, his mind broad, comprehensive,
deep, teeming with thought ; both of sound intellect,
but what a difference of intellectual endowment !   Now
to infuse and foster an ever more and more vigorous
life, to enrich the soul more and more by fresh donations
from the unsearchable riches of Christ, to impart an ever
loftier and holier knowledge of Divine things, so that
the new-born soul may grow up from spiritual infancy
to childhood, from childhood to youth, from youth to
perfect manhood, and be made meet for the inheritance
of the saints in light, this is the design, this the operation of the Holy Ghost in sanctification.

It is no mere self-development ; it is the result of
the eternal purpose of God the Father, of the constant
mediation of Jesus Christ, and of the effectual energy
of the Divine Spirit.   God has predestinated his people
Rom. viii. 29. to be conformed to the image of his Son.   He has
chosen us in Christ before the foundation of the world,
that we should be holy and without blame before him
Ephes. i. 4. in love. He hath from the beginning chosen us to salvation through sanctification of the Spirit and belief of
2 Thess. ii. the truth.   We are " elect according to the foreknow-
13. ledge of God the Father, through sanctification of the
Spirit unto obedience and sprinkling of the blood of
1 Pet. i. 2. Jesus Christ."   It is thus nothing less than the object
of the counsel and workmanship of the Triune Jehovah.

Do any ask why, if the work be gradual and progressive, the apostle writes, " If any man be in Christ,
he is a new creation : old things are passed away ;
2 Cor. v. 17. behold all things are become new ?"   It were enough to
answer by the analogy of the six days' creation : the
darkness passed away, when God said, Let there be

light ; the uniform water-state of our globe passed, when the continents and hills appeared ; the barrenness passed, when the verdure came ; the clouded atmosphere was cleared, when the sun and moon and stars were set for lights in the firmament of heaven ; the ocean and the air were no longer tenantless, when fish and fowl were created ; and the unpeopled land was void no more, when the earth brought forth the living creature after its kind, and God made man in his own image. At any period of this creation you might take your stand and say, Old things had passed away and given place to new ; yet was there an orderly and progressive advancement towards perfection. So is it in the healthy and harmonious process of the new creation (for I am not speaking now of the obstacles and interruptions which man's unbelief may interpose)—just in proportion as we with open face behold as in a glass the glory of the Lord, in like measure shall we all be changed into the same image from glory to glory by the Lord the Spirit.

2 Cor. iii. 18.

This progressive renovation embraces the whole being of man, his body, soul, and spirit, his life before God and his life among his fellow-men. It includes (1) an ever deepening knowledge of the things of God, (2) a growing delight in the heavenly duties of prayer and praise, (3) a more vigorous faith in the salvation of Christ, (4) a more entire submission of our will to God's will, (5) a more resolute crucifying of the flesh and a more earnest cultivation of the fruits of the Spirit, (6) a readier willingness to serve and suffer for our Master here, and (7) a brighter prospect of reigning and rejoicing with him for ever. Suffer me to take up these points one by one.

(1) *Sanctification implies an ever deepening knowledge of the things of God.* This one aspect of sanc-

tification would exhaust an encyclopedia of divinity. I can do little more than sketch its leading features. Whether you regard the subject matter of this heavenly science, or the means provided for acquiring it, or the Great Teacher who undertakes progressively to reveal the mysteries of truth to every childlike disciple, the theme is illimitable. Like the meeting-place of the sea and sky, the loftier the eminence you climb, the farther the horizon seems to recede.

The subject matter is nothing less than the knowledge of God, and of ourselves, and of that kingdom of which he by grace has made us members and inheritors.

" This," says our Lord, " this is life eternal, to know thee, the only true God, and Jesus Christ whom thou John xvii. 3. hast sent." This knowledge of God is to know him in his Divine attributes, as omnipotent, omniscient, omnipresent, and eternal; as the Fountain of life; as that Light in which there is no darkness; as essential Love; as perfect in righteousness and holiness and See Jer. ix. truth; and as infinite in goodness and grace and 24. glory. It is to know him as the Triune Jehovah, God the Father, God the Son, and God the Spirit, in Matt. xxviii. whose name, threefold and yet one, we are baptized. 19. It is to know the Father as reconciling the world unto himself by the incarnation and holy life and atoning death and resurrection and mediation of his dear Son— 2 Cor. v. 19. in a word, to know GOD IN CHRIST. It is to know, by blessed personal experience, what it is to have access by Ephes. ii. 18. one Spirit through Jesus unto the Father. It is to know him now by faith as the Judge of all the earth, and the everlasting King before whom every knee Rom. xiv. 11, shall bow. 12.

In this knowledge the disciple of Christ ought to wax riper and riper. It is true that, when he believed, the believer came to the saving knowledge of the truth: 1 Tim. ii. 4. but this truth has in it breadths, and lengths, and depths, and heights which eternity will not exhaust. This is that heavenly science to which Solomon urges the student to apply his most strenuous endeavours, " My son, if thou wilt incline thine ear unto wisdom and apply thine heart to understanding; yea, if thou criest after knowledge and liftest up thy voice for understanding; if thou seekest her as silver and searchest for her as for hid treasures; then shalt thou understand the fear of the Lord and find the knowledge of God." What intense activity is here! What holy im- Prov. ii. 2—5 portunity! What eager expectancy! How different from the idle, indolent, indifferent supineness to which the flesh would fain resign itself! Truly the highest rewards are offered in Christ's school to the most diligent and successful scholars. This is that advancement of learning, which the apostle pleaded so earnestly the Christians at Colosse might attain, " For which cause," he writes, *i. e.,* having heard of your love in the Spirit, " we do not cease to pray for you, and to desire that ye might be filled with the knowledge of his will in all wisdom and spiritual understanding, that ye might walk worthy of the Lord unto all pleasing, being fruitful in every good work and INCREASING IN THE KNOWLEDGE OF GOD." And if anything could exceed Col. i. 9, 10. the terms of this prayer, it is that which he pours forth for the Ephesians, " That the God of our Lord Jesus Christ, the Father of glory, may give unto you the Spirit of wisdom and revelation in the knowledge of him, the eyes of your heart ($\kappa\alpha\rho\delta\iota\alpha\varsigma$, so all the best MSS.) being enlightened; that ye may know what is the hope of his calling and what the riches of the glory of his inheritance in the saints." These we Ephes. i 17, 18. must ever remember are prayers for the saints and the faithful brethren in Christ. They, like the inspired apostle who wrote to them, had not already attained, neither were they already perfect; and they therefore like him were bound, forgetting those things which were behind and reaching forth unto those which were before, to press toward the mark for the prize of the high calling of God in Christ Jesus.

This knowledge of God involves a corresponding and co-ordinate knowledge of ourselves. Of all subjects of investigation man must needs be the one of most intimate and absorbing interest to man. His understanding susceptible of receiving rays of Divine light varying in intensity from dawn to noonday, his umpire conscience which, as a court of judicature within, passes its verdict on every thought and word and act, his throbbing affections, his enterprising imagination, and his mysterious will which exercises its lordly power over his whole being and is in its highest aspect responsible to the Supreme Will alone; each of these faculties by itself—and all in combination—present almost boundless fields for research. Even a heathen poet could praise

" That heaven-descended maxim, Know THYSELF."

But this self-knowledge, to be of any practical value, is only to be attained in the light of the knowledge of God. Self-loathing is its first result. So Job after his long and severe apprenticeship in the school of suffering says, " I know that thou canst do everything and that no thought can be withheld from thee . . . I have heard of thee by the hearing of the ear but now mine eye seeth thee, wherefore I abhor myself and repent in dust and ashes." So David, who perhaps of all the Old Testament saints knew most of communion with God, lies the lowest before him. Nor needs it to

Job xlii. 2, 5, 6.

Psa. xl. 12.

speak of Peter, Paul, and the beloved John. But this is not all. Every faculty within us, though sinful and sunken and strengthless by reason of the fall, is met by an answering attribute of our Saviour God. In him is light, as we are able to bear it, for our darkened understanding. In him is grace, which sprinkles the guilty conscience with the atoning blood of Jesus and renews its lapsed powers by the Holy Spirit. He is the fontal orb of love, which can shine into the depths of our hearts and awaken every dormant affection there. His promises offer such things, as eye hath not seen nor ear heard, to a hope which his Spirit quickens and sustains. And our wayward and vacillating will is constrained by his Divine good pleasure. Thus we realize more and more the eternal debt of gratitude, which is due to him, who so loved us that where sin abounded grace did much more abound.

And now is the soul free to contemplate that kingdom, of which God by grace has made us members and inheritors. Each living stone is builded into and becomes part of that holy temple, which is built upon the foundation of the apostles and prophets, Jesus Christ himself being the chief corner stone. Each fruitful branch is part of that vine, which is Christ. Each member, even the most feeble, is necessary to the completeness of that mystical body, which is the blessed company of all faithful people. No one liveth and no one dieth to himself. Faith introduces the believer into that whole family in heaven and in earth, which is named after the Father of our Lord Jesus Christ. This glorious truth rightly apprehended is the death-blow of bigotry. It demands largeness of heart, and comprehensiveness of view, and keenness of spiritual vision, and a breadth of affection which can embrace all who love the Lord Jesus Christ in sincerity. For

this is that " mystery of his will, which God, according
to his good pleasure purposed in himself, that in the
dispensation of the fulness of times he might gather
together in one all things in Christ, both which are in
Ephes. i. 9, heaven and which are in earth." So great and high
10.
are the subject-matters of this heavenly science.

The means for acquiring it are commensurate. There
is first the great lesson-book of creation. Here the
student may decypher the alphabet of Divine philosophy. It is his primer. The letters are large and
easy to be understood. The heavens declare the glory
of God, and the firmament showeth his handiwork.
When gazing up into the star-spangled night, who has
not felt with the poet,

" The undevout astronomer is mad?"

Or in the language of inspiration, " When I consider
thy heavens, the work of thy fingers, the moon and the
stars which thou hast ordained, what is man that thou
Psa. viii. 3, 4. art mindful of him ?" And yet that the Lord is
mindful of man, all creation testifies. Mountains and
valleys and plains, the clouds of the air and the precious
droppings of the rain, the glaciers and the everlasting
snows, the well springs, and the rivulets, and the
mighty rivers, the forests and the fruits of the field,
and the luxury of flowers, the oceans which are the
highways of traffic, and the deep mines with their
stored-up treasures, all with ten thousand times ten
thousand voices testify, " The earth is full of the goodness of the Lord ; and so is the great and wide sea
Psa. xxxiii. also." All things proclaim, " Jehovah is a great God
5, and civ.
25. and a great king above all gods : in his hands are all
the deep places of the earth, and the strength of the
hills is his also : the sea is his and he made it ; and
his hands prepared the dry land. O come let us

worship and bow down: let us kneel before the Lord our Maker." And hence the apostle argues that that Psa. xcv. 3 —6. which may be known of God is manifest even among the heathen, " for God hath showed it to them: for the invisible things of him from the creation of the world are clearly seen, being understood by the things which are made, even his eternal power and Godhead, so that they are without excuse." And if creation Rom. i. 19. 20. thus brings those, who know not God, face to face with the Creator, how much rather may the humble student delight to trace therein the footprints of his Father and his God, for—

> His are the mountains, and the valleys his,
> And the resplendent rivers : his to enjoy
> With a propriety that none can feel,
> But who, with filial confidence inspired,
> Can lift to heaven an unpresumptuous eye,
> And smiling say, " My Father made them all."
>
> *Cowper's Task*, book v.

Again there is the second lesson book of Providence. Here the lessons are harder, the rules of interpretation deeper, the apparent anomalies more frequent, the intricacies of heavenly design amid all the perverseness of fallen man far more difficult to unravel. Yet even here, amid all the discordant elements of this sinful world, the voice of God in his dealings with mankind is heard, " Say ye to the righteous, that it shall be well with him, for they shall eat the fruit of their doings. Woe unto the wicked ! it shall be ill with him ; for the reward of his hands shall be given him." This broad Isa. iii. 10, 11 ; see also Eccles. viii. 12, 13. and general lesson is almost forced on the conscience of the world, but the patient disciple in Christ's school, as he reverently bends over the chart of Providence, learns far more of the mysterious ways of God. His faith may often be sorely tried, as was the Psalmist's ; Psa. lxxiii. 2—17. but he knows that God is working all things after the counsel of his own will; he knows that all things shall work together for good to those that love God; he knows that Christ must reign, until he has put all things under his feet: and, though it be but dimly, he forecasts the advent of that everlasting kingdom which can never be shaken. The study itself is of intense and absorbing interest, and the history of the past and the unfolding events of our own days supply an almost boundless field for its pursuit.

But the written word of God is the grand medium of revealing to us his will and ways. It penetrates the ages of a past eternity, and unveils the glories of that which is to come. It opens out to our adoring view the mysteries of the Divine Name. It lays bare the most secret workings of the human heart. It reveals the Father: it testifies of the Son: it bears witness of the Spirit. It unfolds the glorious chart of our redemption and salvation. It is history, and law, and poetry, and oratory, and parable, and promise, and prophecy. Saints without number have drawn thence the water of life, but the fountain-springs well up as unexhausted and inexhaustible as ever. He that meditates therein day and night is like the tree planted by the rivers, and never has it been known for his leaf to wither, nor his branches to cease from yielding fruit.

And to this must be added all those means of grace, which the Lord has provided in such rich abundance for his people, for their better understanding of his lively oracles, and for their growth in the heavenly life—such as Christian friendship, the communion of saints, the courts of prayer, the ministry of the everlasting Gospel, the commemoration of his dying love at his table. No provision on his part is wanting. All things are ready.

Such being the subject matter of this sacred science,

CHAP. VIII.

and such the means for its acquirement, the Teacher is none else than God himself, even the Eternal Spirit which proceedeth from the Father; and is given through the mediation of the Lord Jesus Christ. Thus it was God dealt with Israel in the wilderness, "Thou gavest thy good Spirit to instruct them." This was his invitation by the lips of Solomon, "I will pour out my Spirit unto you, I will make known my words unto you." And this was the great promise of our Lord to his apostles, "Howbeit when he, the Spirit of truth, is come, he will guide you into all the truth ($\pi \hat{a} \sigma a \nu$ $\tau \dot{\eta} \nu$ $\dot{a} \lambda \dot{\eta} \theta \epsilon \iota a \nu$, *i. e.*, all that truth of which he is the Author and Giver—the whole counsel of God); for he shall not speak of himself ($\dot{a} \phi'$ $\dot{\epsilon} a \upsilon \tau o \hat{\upsilon}$, *i. e.*, independently of, or contrary to, the Father and the Son): but whatsoever he shall hear (*i.e.*, from the Father and the Son) shall he speak." Comparing these last words with our Lord's previous declarations regarding himself, "I speak those things which I have heard of him—as the Father hath taught me, I speak," this completes the Divine testimony to the perfect and infinite union of the Father, Son, and Spirit, in the counsel of redemption and in the revelation of that counsel to man. But our Lord continues: "And he will show you things to come:* he shall glorify me, for he shall receive of mine ($\dot{\epsilon} \kappa$ $\tau o \hat{\upsilon}$ $\dot{\epsilon} \mu o \hat{\upsilon}$, collectively, the aggregate of the unsearchable riches of Christ) and shall show it unto you: all things ($\pi \acute{a} \nu \tau a$ $\ddot{o} \sigma a$, distributively, the parts which make up the whole) that the Father hath are mine: therefore said I, that he shall take of mine and shall show it unto you." Again, comparing the words, "He shall glorify me" with the prayer, "Father, glorify thy Son, that thy Son also may glorify thee;" what a glimpse

Nehem. ix. 20.

Prov. i. 23.

John xvi. 13 —15.

See John vii. 17, 18.

ch. vii. 26, 28.

John xvii. 1.

* See Section 7, p. 171.

is here vouchsafed us of the co-equal, co-essential, co-eternal love, communion, and glory of the Triune Jehovah! And into this shrine of ineffable bliss we are admitted by the Comforter, the Spirit of truth, who takes of those "all things" which the Father hath, those "all things" which constitute the boundless inheritance of the Son, and reveals them to us progressively, as we are able to bear them here, and will reveal them in the ages of eternity hereafter.

To this agree the wonderful words of the apostle, "The Spirit searcheth all things, yea the depths of God: for what man knoweth the things of a man, save the spirit of man which is in him? even so the things of God knoweth no one ($o\dot{v}\delta\epsilon\acute{\iota}s$) but the Spirit of God: now we have received not the Spirit of the world, but the Spirit which is of God that we might know the things which are freely given to us of God." And so when he prays that we may climb the loftiest mountain ranges of Divine knowledge, or soar, higher yet, as on eagle's wings, into the pure limitless firmament of Divine love, he relies only upon the illuminating grace of the Spirit of wisdom and revelation, and upon his enabling might strengthening the inner man for this sublimest endeavour.

1 Cor. ii. 10 —12.

Ephes. i. 17; iii. 16—19.

Is the Holy Spirit such a teacher and guide? Is he promised to all who ask? Does he dwell in our hearts? O wherefore are we content with such low attainments and such meagre proficiency in the school of Christ? If a human teacher of vast and varied learning, whose erudition was only equalled by his condescending kindness, were to sojourn a week under our roof, how should we reproach ourselves if we suffered day after day to pass by, and only caught by chance a few golden sentences from his lips, scarcely inviting his communications, or tarrying to receive the rich stream of thought, which he was ever ready to pour into the patient and trustful ear! And if that, which he was most willing to impart, was most essential for our well-being and advancement in life and for our work among our fellow-men, should we not say that, in so scantly improving the irrevocable hours, we were doing ourselves and them much wrong? The parable explains itself.

(2) *Sanctification implies a growing delight in the heavenly duties of prayer and praise.*

From his birthday of living union with Christ, the believer's life is a life of prayer. This is the earliest description of saints, "Then began men to call on the name of the Lord." The promise of salvation is annexed to prayer: "Whosoever shall call on the name of the Lord shall be saved." And this is the apostle's comprehensive definition of the church of God, "All that in every place call upon the name of Jesus Christ our Lord." And the longer we walk by faith, and the nearer we draw to glory, so much the closer ought to be the delightful communion of prayer and praise. Gen. iv. 26.

Joel ii. 32; Acts ii. 21.

1 Cor. ii. 2.

But yet I think there are few complaints more general among Christians than that of *difficulty in prayer*. There is the difficulty of realizing we have free access to God in Christ. There is the difficulty of awakening real desires for heavenly things. There is the difficulty of expressing those desires in words if required, or of connecting those desires with even the most beautiful words where they are expressed. There is the difficulty of putting away wandering thoughts— that bane of devotion. There is the difficulty of grasping the promises. And, lastly, there is the difficulty of watching for an answer. So great and sore are these hindrances, that they wonderfully add to the temptation of not redeeming time for prayer. When

John xiv. 14.

we read, "If ye shall ask anything in my name I will do it," the marvel is that we are not continually at the throne of grace. The devil knows well that prayer is the secret of our strength. Hence he aggravates every difficulty; and if we try to overcome him in our own might, we shall fail. Our devotions will be poor and powerless; our life will become languid; and our service will grievously suffer.

But, blessed be God, we are not left to ourselves. Stronger is He that is with us than he that is with the world. There is a mighty, an almighty Helper, the tenderness of whose sympathy is only equalled by the tenacity of his enduring love, and his gracious office it is to teach and to enable us to pray. He is called "the

Zech. xii. 10.

Spirit of grace and of supplications," as the One who by his secret influence touches the springs of thought within us, quickens desires into life, and encourages and enables us to breathe forth those desires, whether expressed in words or not, into the ear of Eternal Love. And so the apostle writes, "Likewise the Spirit also helpeth ($\sigma\upsilon\nu\alpha\nu\tau\iota\lambda\alpha\mu\beta\acute{\alpha}\nu\epsilon\tau\alpha\iota$) our infirmities, for we know not what to pray for as we ought; but the Spirit itself maketh intercession for us with groanings which cannot be uttered: but ($\delta\acute{\epsilon}$) he that searcheth the hearts knoweth what is the mind of the Spirit, because he maketh intercession for the saints according to the will

Rom. viii. 26, 27.

of God." The word translated "helpeth" signifies to lay hold of anything, as of a beam or burden, together with another. In ourselves we know not what to pray for, or how to pray. But "the Holy Spirit of God dwelling in us, knowing our wants better than we, himself pleads in our prayers, raising us to higher and holier desires than we can express in words, which can

Alford.

only find utterance in sighs and aspirations." But although these yearnings are inexpressible in words, the

Searcher of hearts recognizes in them what is the minding of the Spirit, because these inarticulate pleadings of the Holy Ghost in and for his saints are in perfect unison with his own mind (κατὰ Θεόν)—they are Godlike.

This spirit of prayer, infused and sustained by the Holy Spirit, will interpenetrate our whole life, our life towards God and man. "But ye, beloved," writes St. Jude, " building up yourselves on your most holy faith, PRAYING IN THE HOLY GHOST, keep yourselves in the love of God, looking for the mercy of our Lord Jesus Christ unto eternal life." Do we find it hard to realize our Jude 20, 21. freedom of access to the throne of grace ? let us plead for the ready help of the Spirit, and that Divine court of audience so gloriously pictured will be open to the Heb. iv. 14 – eye of faith, our Father inviting us to draw nigh, and 16. our Advocate pleading for us, and offering with our poor prayers the much incense of his merits upon the golden altar before the throne. Do we find it hard to realize our inestimable privilege in drawing near to God as his children in Christ Jesus ? it is the Spirit of his Son in our hearts, who must cry Abba, Father, until we, by the same Spirit of adoption, imitate the voice of trustful love. Compare Gal. iv. 6 with Rom. viii. 14—17, and observe in the first it is said, *the Spirit cries* Abba, Father, in the second, *we cry;* for he prompts the filial cry, until we learn and repeat it, as infant children learn to lisp a parent's name. Do we find it hard to grasp the promises made to prayer ? let us remember whose sword the Scripture is, even the sword of the Spirit, and wielding it in his might we shall be more than conquerors.

And so with respect to the life of prayer in the midst of our daily work. Our Lord bids us always pray, and not faint. St. Paul urges, "Pray without ceasing." Luke xviii. 1. 1 Thess. v. 17.

But there is only one way to sustain this constant dependence upon God. We must "pray always, with all Ephes. vi. 18. prayer and supplication IN THE SPIRIT." Then shall we realize that our appointed work is that which our Heavenly Father has chosen for us, to prove us, and to humble us, and to train us for glory. Then will conscientiousness in little things be no longer irksome, but be what it is designed to be, a delicate test of love. Then will our daily duties be a help, not a hindrance to our walk with God. To fallen man the pressure downwards of things seen and temporal is constant: the pressure upwards must be constant too. This can only be by the Holy Spirit sustaining communion with God. And the promise is, he shall abide with you for ever—not in hours of private prayer or public worship only, but in the work of the house and of the field, in the bustle of the mart and the vicissitudes of professional life, in the pursuit of science and philosophy, and in bearing an allotted part in the splendours of rank or royalty—wherever his servants are, there is he.

(3) *Sanctification implies a more and more vigorous faith in the salvation of Christ.*

St. Paul, in his first epistle to the Thessalonians, had assured them that he remembered without ceasing their work of faith and labour of love; but in his second epistle he says, "We are bound to thank God always for you, brethren, as it is meet, because your faith groweth exceedingly (ὑπεραυξάνει), and the love of 2 Thess. i. 3. every one of you all toward each other aboundeth." It is not enough to be believers, we must be growing believers. Faith is life; but Jesus came that we might have life, and have it more abundantly. There is a faith, which touches the hem of Christ's garment behind. There is a faith, which implores the laying-on of his healing hand. There is a faith, which sits at his feet, and hears his words. There is a faith, which comes up out of the wilderness, leaning on her Beloved.

Now if we would be joyful and fruitful Christians we must gain this full assurance of faith. I do not say that it is essential to salvation ; for, doubtless, many diffident and trembling saints have entered, are entering, and will enter the gates of glory ; but it is essential to comfort and vigour and strenuous work.

The word translated *full assurance* ($\pi\lambda\eta\rho o\phi o\rho\iota a$) of faith may be best understood by comparing it with its Heb. x. 22. use, where we read of Abraham, "He staggered not at the promise of God through unbelief, but was strong in faith, giving the glory to God, and being fully persuaded ($\pi\lambda\eta\rho o\phi o\rho\eta\theta\epsilon\iota\varsigma$) that what he had promised Rom. iv. 21. he was able also to perform." And as Abraham argued regarding the promised birth of Isaac, so the believer argues in the confidence of faith, " I am as certain as I am of my own existence that the Father sent the Son to be the Saviour of the world, and that Jesus Christ has wrought out a full, free, and finished salvation, and that whosoever believeth on him shall not perish, but have eternal life. I have accepted God's salvation on God's terms. I have cast my guilty self into the arms of Jesus Christ. Other confidences suggest themselves : I will have none of them : I build on Christ, and Christ alone. I have committed my all to him. I have chosen for eternity. This is not nature : it is grace : it is the work of the Holy Spirit in my heart. What follows ? Is it not written, ' Believe on the Lord Jesus Christ, and thou shalt be saved ?' Then I am *saved*—I take the word in all its fathomless fulness of meaning—*saved* from the guilt and tyrannic dominion of sin ; saved from the power of death, and Satan, and hell ; *saved*, so that I may enjoy here the liberty wherewith Christ has made me free, and may hereafter attain the liberty of the glory of the children of God."

It is this assurance of faith which makes its own the certainties of Scripture, saying with Job, "I know that my Redeemer liveth," and with Paul, "I know whom I have believed, and am persuaded He is able to keep that which I have committed to him against that day." And again, "We know that all things work together for good to them that love God." And yet again, "We know that if our earthly house of this tabernacle were dissolved, we have a building of God, an house not made with hands, eternal in the heavens." And with the aged and beloved John, " It doth not yet appear what we shall be, but we know that when he shall appear we shall be like him, for we shall see him as he is."

It is the heart, which is thus enlarged and set at liberty, which runs the way of God's commandments. And this delightful freedom is the work of the Holy Ghost, for " where the Spirit of the Lord is, there is liberty." If, therefore, as we ponder the joy and strength of assurance, our very hearts re-echo the desire of the apostles, " Lord, increase our faith," let us plead anew and with fresh earnestness a prayer dear to many from most sacred associations: "Defend, O Lord, us thy servants with thy heavenly grace, that we may continue thine for ever, and daily increase in thy Holy Spirit more and more, until we come unto thy everlasting kingdom."

(4) *Sanctification implies a more and more entire submission of our will to God's will.*

Although in our Divine Master his will was from everlasting in perfect and harmonious union with the will of his heavenly Father, yet the manifestation of that union and the submission of the Filial to the Paternal will, in prospect of the stupendous work of redemption, and in the midst of the most unparalleled

Marginal references:
Job xix. 25.
2 Tim. i. 12; Rom. viii. 28; 2 Cor v. 1.
1 John iii. 2.
Psa. cxix. 32.
2 Cor. iii. 17.
Luke xvii. 5

sufferings and anguish of spirit, are among the deepest lessons of the word of God. Take but three stand-points of observation. "When he cometh into the world he saith, Sacrifice and offering thou wouldest not, but a body hast thou prepared me . . . then said I, Lo I come; in the volume of the book it is written of me, I delight to do thy will, O my God." In the Heb. x. 5, 7. midst of his laborious ministry he said, "I came down from heaven, not to do mine own will, but the will of him that sent me." And in the unfathomable agonies John vi. 38. of Gethsemane "he prayed, saying, O my Father, if this cup may not pass from me, except I drink it, thy will be done." So it was with him, who has left us an Matt. xxvi. example to follow in his steps; though he was a Son, yet 42. learned he obedience by the things which he suffered. Heb. v. 8. Now as he was, so are we in this world. We have seen in the last chapter, that the self-surrender of our will to the will of God is one of the essential proofs of the new birth of the soul by the power of the Holy Ghost. And often, in the first glow of feeling and affection, there is a peculiar freshness of delight in subordinat-ing our will to the will of him whom our soul loveth. But this obedience will be sorely tried and tested in the long discipline of life. To do, not our own will, but our Father's, involves the taking up the cross daily and bearing it after Jesus—yea, it often implies the surrender of that which is nearest and dearest, when the heart is bleeding at every pore, and the lips can only faintly repeat the words, "If it be possible, let this cup pass from me: nevertheless not as I will but as thou wilt." And this Christlike submission is only to be attained as "we with unveiled face, behold-ing as in a glass the glory of the Lord, are changed into the same image from glory to glory as by the Lord the Spirit."

2 Cor. iii. 18.

(5) *Sanctification implies a more and more resolute crucifying of the flesh and a more and more earnest cultivation of the fruits of the Spirit.*

On this momentous subject the testimony of Scripture is most full and explicit, especially in those two fundamental passages which treat of the Christian's warfare and victory.

Let me touch on the briefest first.

St. Paul is describing the beautifully balanced freedom of the gospel, equally aloof from carnal passions and selfish independence, and continues : " I say then, walk in the Spirit (Πνεύματι, the absence of the article only indicates that the word is regarded as a proper name), and ye shall not fulfil the lust of the flesh." Listen to the voice of the Holy Spirit, follow where he leads, yield to all his gracious influences, for he is waging a mighty conflict in your heart against the flesh. " The flesh," *i.e.*, your corrupt carnal nature, " lusteth against the Spirit," *i.e.*, against the Holy Spirit who has quickened your spirit to life, " and the Spirit against the flesh : for (γάρ, so the best MSS.) these are contrary the one to the other, so that ye do not (ἵνα μή, the result of the antagonism being that ye do not, or tending to prevent you doing) the things that ye would," *i.e.*, those things which your better will desires. Such is the severity of the conflict ye will fail, unless ye walk by the Spirit. " But if ye are led by the Spirit ye are not under the law :" ye are free alike from its bondage and condemnation. We must not for a moment pervert this Scripture, as if it pleaded any excuse for our failures and falls because of the weakness of our fallen nature. There is always in every conflict sufficient grace for us in the Holy Spirit, whereby we may overcome indwelling sin. Only let us seek his grace, only let us yield to his guidance, only let us con ·

Gal. v. 16—26; Rom. vii. 14, to viii. 17.

Gal. v. 16—26.

ver. 17.

tend in his might: and we may, we must conquer. This Scripture is not apologetic, but animating. But having declared of the flesh and the Spirit, these are contrary the one to the other, the apostle proves it by placing (ver. 19—23) the dark and disastrous works of the flesh side by side with the beautiful and blessed fruits of the Spirit. The works of the flesh which he enumerates may be grouped in four classes—sensuality, impiety, malignity, self-indulgence. And having contrasted with these the heavenly fruits of the Spirit, he adds (v. 24), "Now they that are Christ's crucified (ἐσταύρωσαν, aorist) the flesh with its passions and lusts." It is true that it is a lingering death which the flesh dies, but they who are Christ's, when they believed, began through the Spirit to mortify the deeds of the body. "If we live by the Spirit,"—for the conflict described above bespeaks one whose soul is quickened to spiritual life—the dead in sin do not fight against sin—"let us also walk (στοιχῶμεν, yet stronger than περιπατεῖτε in the 16th verse, and implying a more studied following of a prescribed course) by the Spirit." This holy, consistent, spiritual walk will alone deliver us from the thorny and dangerous by-paths of ambition, emulation, and envy.

The believer's life-long conflicts and final victory are described more at length in Rom. vii. 14 to viii. 17.[*]

St. Paul (ch. vii. 7—13) had been referring to the days of his childhood and early youth, before he was at all conscious of the claims of the law, and when he imagined all was well with him as a dutiful son of Abraham. But with unfolding manhood the law grappled more powerfully with his conscience ; it demanded unfaltering obedience ; it met the resistance of the

---

* See note, Preface, page ii.

unsubdued will. And thus when "the commandment came,", and found him out, "sin revived" from its death-like torpor; "but I," says the apostle, "died," seeing that I had incurred the penalty of the broken law, so that the dreams of my own goodness vanished away, and my peace and hope utterly perished under the withering sentence, "Dying, thou shalt die." The violated commandment was my death-warrant. This conflict in his breast, before he knew Christ, only illustrated the spotless purity of the law, and yet its powerlessness to sanctify the heart and life through the exceeding sinfulness of man. But this was not all. The conflict waged before the imparting of the grace of God had been continued since. From verse 7th to verse 13th the apostle had been speaking in the past tense, describing throughout his state as an unregenerate Pharisee. At the 14th verse he notably changes to the present tense, and speaks in that tense of his own experience to the end of the 25th verse, describing his state of warfare, since he became a Christian and an apostle. What, then, is the testimony of this later conflict, in which the new man contends with the old, as to the holiness of the Divine law and the sinfulness of the carnal mind? It is still the same. The law is just and good; but it has not power *in itself*, when the struggling saint looks to it instead of looking to Christ and his Spirit, to overcome indwelling sin.

This inbred corruption is a powerful and rebellious vassal, who, though driven from the throne of the heart and in process of subjugation, is not yet wholly expelled the kingdom, and sometimes obtains a temporary but disastrous victory. And under the deep sense of the utter depravity of the old nature, of the bitterness of the conflict, and of the misery of even an occasional defeat in this warfare, the apostle exclaims, "O wretched

man that I am!" and longs with intense desire for perfect emancipation "from the body of this death," the
body in which to the very last this sore fight must be
fought, and which must itself, ere the final victory,
succumb to the curse of the broken law.

But in pondering this passage of holy writ we must
be careful to remember, that this is a description of
what the believer's struggles practically are, and not of
what his victories, so far as the promises of the gospel
are concerned, always might be. He is often weak: he
might be always strong. He is often groaning: he
might be always rejoicing. He is often baffled: he
might be always triumphant. We must never use
St. Paul's argument here to excuse our failures and
falls, as if we could not stand in Christ's might. This
would be indeed to dishonour the Spirit of grace. We
fail, not because there is not ample strength in Jesus
Christ for us, but because in our folly and sin we are
trusting in ourselves to obey the law. And the law
cannot sanctify us. It can communicate no vital power.
It can generate no love. Hence our mournful defeats.
But whenever we look to Christ, and just in proportion
as we look to Christ, and depend upon the aid of his
Spirit, we are made more than conquerors through him
who loved us. This the eighth chapter proceeds to unfold.

By our union with Christ Jesus we are made partakers of the life-giving Spirit of Christ. The Divine
Spirit which Christ gives quickens and animates the
human spirit. And the believer, just in proportion as
he is obedient to this new principle of action, this code
of love, which the apostle calls "the law of the Spirit
of life," is set free from the law of sin and death.
St. Paul had fully admitted the wretchedness of the
captivity into which sin sometimes brought the believer;
but he proceeds to dwell upon the prevalent liberty

which the Holy Spirit enabled him to enjoy, a liberty which was always his privilege and generally his attainment. The characteristic description of believers is, " Those who walk not after the flesh but after the Spirit."

Wherein this broad distinction consists he goes on to explain. "They, who are (*i.e.*, live) after the flesh, mind ($\phi\rho o\nu o\hat{u}\sigma\iota\nu$) the things of the flesh"—the prevalent bent and bias of their desires are towards carnal things, the drift of their life is towards the world— " whereas those, who are after the Spirit, mind the things of the Spirit"—the prevalent aim and object with them is the cultivation of that spiritual life, which has been quickened and is fostered by the Holy Spirit; the current of their being sets to Godward. The courses are contrary one to another: the issues are contrary likewise. Nor need we marvel at this vast difference. The minding of the flesh must be ruin, because "it is hatred towards God," and for man, the creature, to hate God, the Creator, must end in death. But ye, believers, " are not in the flesh (in the sense of living after the flesh), but in the Spirit," *i e.*, you live after the Spirit: "if, at least, the Spirit of God dwells in you." As if he would say. search your hearts—it is not the name of Christians, but the indwelling of the Divine Spirit which constitutes the spiritual man. This proviso is essential, "for, if any man have not the Spirit of Christ, he is none of his." What a solemn undertone of warning this solemn parenthesis supplies! "And if Christ be in you"— you being one with Christ by the indwelling of his Spirit,—"whereas your body is dead because of sin (*i.e.*, as explained ch. vi. 11, ye died with Christ, and thus are called to regard the members of your body as dead unto sin), the spirit," *i.e.*, your spirit renewed by the Holy Ghost, " is life because of righteousness." Ye rose with Christ, who is your justifying righteousness, Ephes. ii. 5, 6. and imparts to you sanctifying righteousness, and will, when he your life appears, clothe you with glorifying righteousness.

Now ye are alive to God. The Spirit of God the Father, who raised up Jesus from the dead, dwells in you : this (ver. 11 : see this verse unfolded in the following chapter of this treatise) insures your future resurrection life.

" We therefore are debtors not to the flesh." The debtor is servant to the creditor : our debt is cancelled ; we are free ; we owe no allegiance to the flesh, but to the Spirit. " For if ye live after the flesh, ye shall die "—this your apparent life is the road to death; a death incipient here, ratified in Hades, and consummated in eternity—" but if ye by the Spirit (the Spirit of God acting upon your spirit) do put the deeds of the body to death, ye shall live," a life beginning now, confirmed in Paradise, and perfected in glory.

Nor let the believer be staggered at the confident assurance—*ye shall live.* " For, as many as are led by God's Spirit, they are God's sons." I say *sons,* " for " when ye believed in Christ " ye received not the spirit of bondage again to (εἰς, " leading to ") fear. Once ye were bond-servants to the flesh : the Spirit of Christ, however, brought you into no second (πάλιν) bondage. But ye received the Spirit of sonship, through whom (*i. e.,* by whose grace and power) we cry, Abba, Father "—the Hebrew and Greek forms pointing to the fact that both Jew and Gentile have through Christ a common access by one Spirit unto the Father. Yea more : this our filial relationship to God, which prompts ver. 16. the cry Abba, Father, is attested and confirmed by the Holy Spirit, ratifying the assurance of our own spirit that we are the children of God. But the fact that we are children involves the certainty of an inheritance. God has no portionless sons. " We are heirs of God," as our Father from whom we receive our portion, " and joint-heirs with Christ," who is himself Heir of all things, but freely shares all things with those, whom John xvii. 22. he is not ashamed to call his brethren. Do any object that our present trials negative such blessed hopes? Nay, the sufferings are a pledge of the glory in reversion. The Heir of all things suffered, ere he sat down on the right hand of the Majesty on High. We now share his sufferings—we shall share his glory.

In both these momentous passages of Holy Writ we learn that the work of the Divine Spirit in the heart consists, not only in crucifying the old man, but equally and coincidently in forming and nurturing the new. Sanctification is no dreary negative; it leaves no aching void ; it is a well of water springing up to everlasting life. Thus, in Gal. v. 16—26, after the description of the works of the flesh, which the believer renounces, how blessed is the contrast drawn by the apostle of the free and spontaneous fruit of the Spirit— love, joy, peace, long-suffering, gentleness, goodness, faith, meekness, temperance ! It is like the fruit tree yielding fruit after its kind, whose seed is in itself. Love stands first, as " the chiefest " of all graces; but the rest seem rather presented to us in that rich and luxuriant profusion, the abundance of which is magnified by the absence of systematic arrangement. They who searched Canaan of old, we read, " cut down from the brook of Eschol a branch with one cluster of grapes, and bare it between two upon a staff, and brought of the pomegra-

Numb. xiii. 23.

nates and of the figs " to their brethren in the wilderness. This heavenly fruit may be to us, every day of our earthly pilgrimage, a foretaste of the promised land.

And so in Rom. vii. 14 to viii. 17, it is not only the bitter conflict against the sin that dwelleth in us, and the stern mortification of the deeds of the body, but it is the delighting in the law of God after the inward man, it is with the mind serving the law of God, it is walking after the Spirit, it is minding the things of the Spirit—a spiritual-mindedness, which is life and peace, it is being led by the Spirit of God, it is the having the Spirit of adoption, whereby we cry Abba, Father, and it is the hearing the secret witness of the Spirit with our spirit that we are the children of God. Here is a positive life, a pledge and foretaste of eternal life which infinitely transcends all the transient joys of the world. They, who thus sow to the Spirit, are sowing a harvest of everlasting felicity. Only may we remember, he that soweth sparingly shall reap sparingly, and he that soweth bountifully shall reap also bountifully. With this the next division of my subject is closely allied.

(6) *Sanctification implies an ever readier willingness to serve and suffer for our Master here.*

Christianity is faith and love and hope ; but it is no lifeless faith, no idle love, no foolish hope which makes the aspirant ashamed. Nay, rather it is known as " the work of faith, the labour of love, the patience of hope." And so we always find in Scripture that the spiritual man is expected to be ready for service, or, if need be, for suffering. The law, the Psalms, and the prophets with one voice enforce the practical goodness of the children of God. Their names testify of this : they are not only called the godly, the wise in heart, the Lord's hidden ones ; but the righteous, the upright, the perfect, the just, the good. This spirit of holiness breathes in all the discourses of our Lord. The epistles, after treating of the highest and holiest doc-

1 Thess. i. 3.

trines, continually descend to the humblest duties of every-day life. Let Rom. xii., xiii.; 1 Cor. xv. 58, xvi. 1; 2 Cor. vii. 1; Gal. vi. 1—10; Ephes. iv.—vi.; Phil. iv. 8, 9; Col. iii., iv.; 1 Thess. iv. 1—11; 2 Thess. iii. 6—13; the practical directions so profusely scattered in the pastoral epistles to Timothy and Titus; Heb. xii. 1; James i. 22; 1 Pet. ii. 11; iii. 16; 2 Pet. iii. 11—14; 1 John ii. 3, iii. 7, 18, v. 4, bear witness, what is that holy and just and blameless walk before God and man, which the Gospel demands. And in the book of Revelation this stands as one of the latest messages of the Son of God to his Church, " Behold, I come quickly, and my reward is with me, to give every man according as his work shall be."

Rev. xxii. 12.

Now it needs but to turn to the first chapter of this treatise, and glance over the Scripture testimony there adduced, to see how every good thought and word and work is ascribed to God, and to the operation of His Spirit. No one could rise from the study of this subject without exclaiming, with Isaiah, " Thou, Lord, hast wrought all our works in us." He works invisibly in us both to will and to do of his good pleasure. Yea, this power of the Holy Ghost was that, which without measure abode upon the Son of Man himself, and enabled him for his mighty ministry and service. God, we read, anointed him with the Holy Ghost and with power. And from his incarnation to his ascension, the Christ lived, and laboured, and suffered, and triumphed in the power of the Holy Ghost. And so has it been with his servants both under the elder and later dispensations. The expression in the original is worthy of note, " The Spirit of the Lord CLOTHED Gideon." " Then the Spirit CLOTHED Amasai." " The Spirit of God CLOTHED Zachariah." They were clad in power both for action and utterance by the Holy Ghost.

Isa. xxvi. 12.

Phil. ii. 13.

Acts x. 38.

Judg. vi. 34.

1 Chron. xii. 18.

2 Chron. xxiv. 20.

And when the Great Head of his Church was about to leave her in the wilderness for a time, this was his latest promise to his apostles, and to them as examples of all who should testify to the truth in every age, " Ye shall receive power after that the Holy Ghost is come upon you, and ye shall be witnesses for me." Acts i. 8. The Gospel in the lips of the ministers of Christ must be in demonstration of the Spirit and of power— yea, for this very reason is the treasure in earthen vessels, that the excellency of the power may be seen to be of God and not of man. This enables them to speak 1 Cor. ii. 4; in the Spirit, not of cowardice (δειλίας), but of power 2 Cor. iv. 7 and of love and of a sound mind. And in all the manifold diversities of gifts which obtain in the church militant here on earth, it is that one and the self-same Spirit who worketh all in all, dividing to every man severally as he wills. His extraordinary and miraculous gifts have indeed been withdrawn from us, as no longer necessary since the canon of Scripture was completed; but his ordinary gifts, comprising everything needful for the government and administration of his church, and for the life and godliness of every member of the same, are as freely and richly dispensed by him as ever. And it is as true now as in the apostolic age, that " as the body is one, and hath many members, and all the members of that one body, being many, are one body, so also is Christ: for by one Spirit are we all baptized into one body, whether we be Jews or Gentiles, whether we be bond or free, and have been all made to drink into one Spirit." Thus the humblest 1 Cor. xii. 13. offices, as the highest, are dependent for their right 14. exercise on that rich dowry of gifts, which our risen Head received, when he ascended up on high, and led captivity captive, and gave gifts to men,—our Head, even Christ, from whom the whole body, fitly joined

together, and compacted by that which every joint sup-
plieth, making increase of the body unto the edifying

See Ephes. iv. 7—15.

of itself in love.

And as with service so is it with suffering. Our
great High Priest in all that he endured for us, from
the opening of his ministry, when after his baptism he
was led up of the Spirit into the wilderness to be
tempted of the devil, even to its patient close, when he
through the Eternal Spirit offered himself without spot
to God, suffered, as he served, in the power of the
Holy Ghost. The corn was bruised; and the offering

Lev. ii. 1, etc.

of fine flour was ever mingled with oil and frankincense.
Herein has he left us an example, that we should
follow in his steps. "Beloved," writes St. Peter, "think
it not strange concerning the fiery trial which is to try
you, as though some strange thing happened unto you,
but rejoice inasmuch as ye are partakers of Christ's
sufferings; that when his glory shall be revealed, ye
may be glad also with exceeding joy: if ye be reproached for the name of Christ, happy are ye, FOR THE

1 Pet. iv. 12 —14.

SPIRIT OF GLORY AND OF GOD RESTETH UPON YOU."
Tears and trials for Christ's sake are the seed of joy,
sufferings of glory, reproaches of everlasting honour.
Even now the Holy Spirit, who is the fountain of all
true glory, seeing that he proceedeth from the Father
of glory and from the Lord of glory (such seems the
force of the beautiful expression, "the Spirit of glory
and of God"), rests upon the suffering saint. The
annals of the church of Christ in its darkest seasons of
tribulation have borne bright and abundant testimony
to the truth of the apostle's words. Our missionary
records bear the same witness. And even in the com-
parative peace of Christian lands who cannot testify,
that in hours of sore trial, and by bedsides of protracted
pain, he has seen the sufferer's face lighted up with

the grace and glory of the Spirit of God? The crushed myrrh has given forth all its sweetness. And the chamber of suffering has been like that spot where Jacob slept—none other than the house of God and the very gate of heaven. And this naturally introduces me to the last point which I named.

(7) *Sanctification implies a bright and brighter prospect of reigning and rejoicing with Christ for ever.*

The promise of our Lord to his apostles regarding the Comforter, "He shall show you things to come," was no doubt largely fulfilled to them personally in miraculous gifts of prophecy, in spiritual revelations of future glory, in historic predictions interspersed through the epistles (such as 2 Thess. ii. 3, 1 Tim. iv. 1, 2 Pet. ii., etc.), and in the crowning apocalyptic visions granted to John in Patmos. But this does not exhaust the meaning of these emphatic words. Every one who is born of the Spirit is taught by him to conceive some hopes of the good things to come. "Being justified by faith," writes the apostle, "we have peace with God through our Lord Jesus Christ, by whom also we have access by faith into this grace wherein we stand, AND REJOICE IN HOPE OF THE GLORY OF GOD." And at the close of the same epistle we are taught who alone can work in us this joyful foretaste in heaven, "Now the God of hope fill you with all joy and peace in believing, that ye may abound in hope through the power of the Holy Ghost." So, likewise while confessing, "Eye hath not seen, nor ear heard, neither have entered into the heart of man the things which God hath prepared for them that love him;" the same apostle continues, "But God hath revealed them unto us by his Spirit, for the Spirit searcheth all things— yea, the deep things of God." And so St. Peter, in

John xvi. 13.

e. g., Acts xi. 28.
e. g., Rom. viii. 14—23.

Rom. v. 1; xv. 13.

1 Cor ii. 9, 10.

writing to those "elect according to the foreknowledge of God the Father, through sanctification of the Spirit unto obedience and sprinkling of the blood of Jesus Christ," immediately breaks forth into adoring praise of him "who hath begotten us again unto a lively hope by the resurrection of Jesus Christ from the dead; to an inheritance incorruptible and undefiled, and that 1 Pet. i. 2—4. fadeth not away, reserved in heaven for us." And, lastly, the beloved John has no sooner spoken of the anointing, which we have received from God, abiding in us and teaching us all things, than he rises from our lofty privilege here as children in the household of faith to the yet loftier dignity, which is before us as the children of the resurrection: "Beloved now are we the sons of God, and it doth not yet appear what we shall be; but we know that, when he shall appear, 1 John ii. 27; we shall be like him, for we shall see him as he is."
iii. 2.

As the issue of the Holy Spirit's work in the church triumphant forms the subject of the last and concluding chapter of this treatise, I do little more now than allude to the blessed fact that he it is, who kindles and fosters and sustains this heavenly hope in those who, by patient continuance in well-doing, seek for glory, and honour, and immortality. And yet, perhaps, in nothing is his progressive work more discernible than in the growing *heavenly-mindedness* of those whom he is training for the kingdom of God. And how often in the last few months of the pilgrim's course have his brethren been constrained to say, We could not be in our brother's company without feeling that he was ripening fast for glory. Not seldom the light beyond seems to stream down through the half-open gates on the last stage of the journey. The saint, when flesh and heart are failing him, not seldom seems to have heaven in his eye and in his heart. And beautiful as was the dewy freshness of the dawn, and strong as was the light and the power of noon, these sunset hues have a peculiar beauty which is all their own—a tender transparency which is not of earth, a richness and a glory which tell of the nearer presence of God.

Such is what may be called the natural and normal process of sanctification in the heart of the believer. Some, however, will complain that " they find neither in themselves nor others, by the best of their observation, that the work of sanctification is constantly progressive, or that holiness doth so grow or thrive, wherever it is in sincerity." But, as Owen so well replies to this objection, " It is one thing what grace or holiness is suited unto in its own nature, and what is the ordinary or regular way of the procedure of the Spirit in the work of sanctification, according to the tenor of the covenant of grace; another, what may occasionally fall out by indisposition and irregularity, or any other obstructing interposition in them in whom the work is wrought. A child that hath a principle of life, a good natural constitution, and suitable food, will grow and thrive; but that which hath obstructions from within, or distempers and diseases, or falls and bruises, may be weak and thriftless. When we are regenerate we are as new-born babes, and ordinarily, if we have the sincere milk of the word, we shall grow thereby. But if we ourselves give way to temptations, corruptions, negligences, conformity to the world, is it any wonder if we are thriftless?"

But be it so, that we have suffered some sudden and lamentable fall, like David or Peter, or that we are conscious of a chronic depression of spiritual life, an apathy and weariness and winter of soul, which makes us cry, with the patriarch, " Oh that I were as in months past, as in the days when God preserved me,

Job xxix. 2, 3.

when his candle shined upon my head, and when by his light I walked through darkness!" Yet let us remember, that it is the gracious office of the Holy Spirit to raise up the fallen, to restore the backslider, and to revive the dry and parched soil with the dews of his forgiving love and mercy. When Samson fell, and his hair—the sign of that Nazarite vow which bound him to the service of God—was shorn, his strength went from him. "Howbeit," we read, "the hair of his head began to grow again after he was shaven;" and by one wrestling and prevalent prayer he obtained

Judg. xvi. 19—28.

strength for his final victory. After his grievous fall the penitent Psalmist prayed, "Cast me not away from thy presence, and take not thy Holy Spirit from me; restore unto me the joy of thy salvation, and uphold me with thy free Spirit; then will I teach transgressors thy ways, and sinners shall be converted unto

Psa. li. 10— 12.

thee." The goodness of Israel had been as the morning cloud; they had fallen by their iniquity; but they are invited to return; and the promise runs, "I will heal their backsliding, I will love them freely: for mine anger is turned away from him. I will be as the dew unto Israel; he shall grow as the lily, and cast forth his roots as Lebanon. His branches shall spread, and his beauty shall be as the olive tree, and his smell as Lebanon. They that dwell under his shadow shall return; they shall revive as the corn, and grow as the vine: the scent thereof shall be as the wine of

Hosea xiv. 4 —7.

Lebanon." What is not here promised to the penitent backslider from the healing and forgiving love of God? —the reviving dews of his Spirit, the purity of the lily, the stability of Lebanon, expansive usefulness, abiding beauty, rich fragrance, and far-reaching influence for good. St. Peter rose the stronger from his fall, and his threefold denial was condoned by the threefold

pastoral commission to feed the lambs and sheep of
Christ's flock. The Corinthians fell into mournful
spiritual pride and other sins; but the Holy Spirit
moved the apostle to write to them that letter of inimi-
table tenderness and faithfulness, and moved them to
receive the rebuke in the love of it. They sorrowed
after a godly sort; and see what carefulness it wrought
in them, yea, what clearing of themselves, yea, what
indignation, yea, what fear, yea, what vehement desire,
yea, what zeal, yea, what revenge! The church of 2 Cor. vii. 11.
Ephesus, notwithstanding all her labours, had left her
first love; but the voice of the Son of Man, walking
amid the seven golden candlesticks, calls upon her to
remember and repent and do the first works. The Rev. ii. 4, 5.
experience of every believer in every age has shed
fresh lustre on that simple clause of the twenty-third
Psalm, "He restoreth my soul."

But this being granted, nevertheless, seeing that it
is the design of God to sanctify us wholly, and to preserve our whole spirit, soul, and body, blameless unto
the coming of our Lord Jesus Christ, how earnestly
should we desire, how persistently should we pray, how
diligently should we strive to grow in grace and in the
knowledge of our Lord and Saviour, to walk with God
in ever closer communion, to hold on and to hold out
in full assurance of faith, to submit more cheerfully
our will to his, to crucify the flesh and cultivate the
fruits of the Spirit more resolutely, to serve or suffer
for our Master with a readier willingness, and to rejoice with a brighter hope in the prospect of his coming
and kingdom. For what is such growth in the Divine
life but the transformation into the image of our Lord,
the becoming more Christ-like, more God-like, the being
made more meet for the inheritance of the saints in
light? This is the seal of the Holy Spirit.

CHAP. VIII.
———

John vi. 27.

When our Lord says of himself, as the Son of Man, " Him hath God the Father sealed," he declares himself to be accredited, by the mighty works which he did in his Father's name and by the power of the Holy Ghost, as the Saviour of the world. When St. Paul writes to the Corinthians, " God hath anointed us, and hath also sealed us, and given the earnest of the Spirit in our hearts," and says to the Ephesians,* " After that ye believed, ye were sealed with that Holy Spirit of promise, which is the earnest of our inheritance until the redemption of the purchased possession," and again, when he charges them, " Grieve not the Holy Spirit of God, whereby ye are sealed unto the day of redemption," he speaks of the Holy Ghost impressing believers with the impress of Christ's image, which is a pledge and earnest whose they are and what is the inheritance laid up for them in heaven. It is true, that in the apostolic age this sealing of the Spirit was often accompanied by miraculous signs, as with the household of Cornelius and the twelve disciples at Ephesus; but although the outward signs are withdrawn, the sealing is none the less real, nor its import as an earnest the less true. And so in the Apocalypse,

2 Cor. i. 21, 22.

Ephes. i. 13, 14; iv. 30.

Acts x. 44— 46; xix. 6.

---

* The allusion to the seal as a pledge of purchase would be peculiarly intelligible to the Ephesians, for Ephesus was a maritime city, and an extensive trade in timber was carried on there by the shipmasters of the neighbouring ports. The method of purchase was this : the merchant, after selecting his timber, stamped it with his own signet, which was an acknowledged sign of ownership. He often did not carry off his possession at the time ; it was left in the harbour with other floats of timber ; but it was chosen, bought, and stamped ; and in due time the merchant sent a trusty agent with the signet, who, finding that timber which bore a corresponding impress, claimed and brought it away for the master's use. Thus the Holy Spirit impresses on the soul now the image of Jesus Christ ; and this is the sure pledge of the everlasting inheritance.

which was vouchsafed to the Church, when the extra-ordinary gifts of the Spirit were about to cease, we read that the hundred and forty and four thousand were sealed with the seal of the living God, that they might be kept amid all the conflicts of the world ; and in a subsequent vision these all appear, not one want-ing, standing with the Lamb on the heavenly Mount Zion, having his name * and the name of his Father written on their foreheads. This Divine image begins to be formed in the heart, when first the soul looks upon Jesus Christ and believes and lives. But the likeness may be more or less vivid, the lineaments ex-pressed in stronger or fainter relief, the progressive transformation more or less decided and manifest to all. May it be ours to draw near by faith continually to him who is the source of life and light and love, and thus, with unveiled face, beholding as in a glass the glory of the Lord, to be changed into the same image, from glory to glory, as by the Lord the Spirit.

Rev. vii. 2–8 ; xiv. 1–3.

---

* In Rev. xiv. i., add τὸ ὄνομα αὐτοῦ καί after ἔχουσαι, with the best MSS., including the Sinaitic.

CHAPTER IX

THE ISSUE OF THE HOLY SPIRIT'S WORK IN THE EVER-LASTING KINGDOM

In the first five chapters of this treatise we have con-sidered the witness of Scripture to the Holy Spirit, his distinct Personality, his eternal Godhead, his unction of the Son of man, and his inspiration of the oracles of God. The foundation having been thus laid, we have in the last three chapters sought to trace, so far as Scripture leads us by the hand, the workings of this same Divine Spirit in the heart of man, his striving with the world, his quickening dead souls to life, and his progressive sanctification of the believer. It remains only, that we should endeavour humbly and reverently to gather up the scattered notices of Holy Scripture regarding the triumph of his beneficent work in the everlasting kingdom of our Lord and Saviour Jesus Christ.

There are some who would foreclose any inquiry into the glories to come by saying, " We are assured that, when we wake after his likeness, we shall be satis-fied : Why need we ask any more ? Is not this enough ?" I would venture to answer, No ; it is not enough, if more is revealed : for, while the hidden things belong to the Lord our God, those things which are revealed belong unto us and to our children (and observe the

CHAP. IX.

practical effect), that we may do all the words of the
law. It is not enough; for "ALL Scripture is given by
inspiration of God, and is profitable for doctrine, for
reproof, for correction, for instruction in righteousness,
that the man of God may be perfect, throughly furnished unto all good works." It is not enough; for
though it is true the apostle says, "Eye hath not
seen nor ear heard, neither have entered into the
heart of man the things which God hath prepared for
them that love him," he continues, "but God hath
revealed them unto us by his Spirit:" nor is this to
be confined to the inspired writers, for St. Paul proceeds to apply this to all who are taught of God,
saying, "We have received the Spirit of God, that we
might know the things which are freely given us of
God . . . but the natural man receiveth not the
things of the Spirit of God, neither can he know them,
because they are spiritually discerned; but he that is
spiritual judgeth all things." And it is not enough,
because of the solemn admonition of St. Peter, "We
have also a more sure word of prophecy, whereunto ye
do well that ye take heed, as unto a light that shineth
in a dark place, until the day dawn and the day star
arise in your hearts."*

Deut. xxix. 29.

2 Tim. iii. 16. 17.

1 Cor. ii. 9– 15.

2 Pet. i. 19.

This, however, being premised, it is most true that
in this inquiry we especially need a cautious reverence
and a docile faith, and, above all, a prayerful dependence
on the teaching of the same Divine Spirit. We need
reverent caution, lest we should rashly intrude into

---

* I would venture to refer the reader to a little work of mine,
entitled "The Risen Saints: what does Scripture reveal of their
Estate and Employments?" where I have given some of the
thoughts expressed in this chapter, and have sought to develop
them more at length from a wider comparison of the exceeding
great and precious promises of the Word.

See Col. ii. 18. things unseen. We need docility of faith, lest haply our Lord should say to us, as to Nicodemus, "If I have told you earthly things, and ye believe not, how John iii. 12. shall ye believe if I tell you of heavenly things?" And we need earnestly to pray for the teaching of the Holy Ghost, for it is the Blessed Comforter's prerogative to ch. xvi. 13. show us things to come.

Let us then consider the issue of the Holy Spirit's work—(1) In the perfection of the glorified saint; (2) In the completion of the Elect Church; (3) In the new heavens and the new earth, wherein dwelleth righteousness.

(1) The glorified saint will be perfect in body, in mind, and in spirit.

The resurrection body will be a perfect instrument for all the functions of the perfectly regenerate spirit. For so we are assured. He will change the body of our humiliation (τὸ σῶμα τῆς ταπεινώσεως ἡμῶν), that it may be fashioned like unto the body of his glory (σύμμορφον τῷ σώματι τῆς δόξης αὐτοῦ), according to the working whereby he is able even to subdue all Phil. iii. 21. things unto himself. We shall be planted together Rom. vi. 5. with him in the likeness of his resurrection. Now our Lord's resurrection body was visible or invisible at his will: it was not corruptible flesh and blood, which St. 1 Cor. xv. 50. Paul assures us cannot inherit the kingdom of God, but it was veritable flesh and bones, the same flesh and bones, though now immortal and incorruptible, which had been nailed to the cross; for our Lord said to his affrighted apostles, "Behold my hands and my feet, that it is I myself; handle me, and see; for a Luke xxiv. 39. spirit hath not flesh and bones, as ye see me have:" though a spiritual body, it was capable of receiving material food, for our Lord took of the broiled fish and ch. xxiv. 43. honeycomb, and ate before them: though tangible, it was not bound to our solid globe, for in that body he ascended till a cloud received him out of their sight; yea, therein he took his seat at the right hand of the Father, far above all principality, and power, and might.

And as it was with Him, so it shall be with us. That which was sown in corruption, dishonour, and weakness shall be raised in incorruption, glory, and power. That which was sown a natural body shall be raised a spiritual body.

There are other helpful illustrations in nature, which are often appealed to in treating of the resurrection, such as the apparent death of spring, followed by the life of spring, the chrysalis and the winged moth, etc.; but this divinely-chosen analogy of the seed and the plant is to me of all the most suggestive regarding our spiritual body as it shall be hereafter. For, take the bulb of a hyacinth, or of any other flower, submit it to a naturalist, and he will tell you, by aid of the microscope, what the perfected flower will be; yet who, that did not know the mysteries of vegetation, could believe that from that dull and dismal bulb would spring that gorgeous flower enveloped in its sheltering leaves? Such, however, shall be our body then compared with our body now: such shall be that building of God, not made with hands, eternal in the heavens, compared with the earthly house of this tabernacle which is awaiting its dissolution. Whether we think of sight, or hearing, or motion, or speech, or any other faculty, we may safely argue, what the flower is to the seed, that shall our enlarged and ennobled powers hereafter be to our narrow and confined capabilities here. It will be an exceeding and eternal weight of glory; for did the risen Lord say of himself, I am the bright

Ephes. i. 20, 21.

1 Cor. xv 42 —44.

2 Cor. v. 1.

and the morning star, and was his countenance as seen

Rev. i. 16; xxii. 16. by St. John like the sun shining in its strength? we are assured that, when the wise awake from the sleep of death, in that day of the manifestation of the sons of Rom. viii. 19. God, they shall shine as the brightness of the firmament, Dan. xii. 2. and as the stars for ever and ever.

Now the Agent employed in the raising up our mortal body to immortal life is expressly declared to be the Holy Ghost; for the apostle says, " If the Spirit of him who raised up Jesus from the dead dwell in you, he that raised up Christ from the dead shall also quicken your mortal bodies by his Spirit that dwelleth Rom. viii. 11. in you." St. Paul's argument is this: Ye are alive unto God: the Spirit of God the Father, who raised up Jesus from the dead, dwells in you: this ensures your resurrection. The one stupendous barrier was that of sin and death. Christ has put away sin; Christ has conquered death: your resurrection is bound up in his: he will not suffer your bodies for ever to see corruption. No, they are the temples of the Holy Ghost. Not in vain has the Blessed Spirit dwelt in that mortal frame of yours, and illuminated that finite mind with heavenly truth, and warmed that human heart with devout affections, and strengthened those hands for his service, and directed those feet in the path of his commandments, and opened those trembling lips to speak of his love. It was an unutterable act of grace in the Father to send the Holy Ghost to visit you in your low estate; but now, seeing the way is opened by the death and resurrection of Jesus Christ, be assured He will quicken your mortal bodies in the last day by the same indwelling Spirit. And then will the body no longer be, as now it so often proves, a weight, a weary weight on the elastic soul within, but rather as eagle-wings to bear us upward into the everlasting sunlight of the love of God.

And as with the body, so with the mind: our mental and intellectual powers will then be perfect. In proof of this it is sufficient to adduce the apostle's argument: 1 Cor. xiii. 8 —12. "Prophecies," he says, "will become useless (καταργη- θήσονται)," for things which are mysteries now will be transparent hereafter; "tongues will cease," for then one song of praise shall rise from the universe of God, and therefore one language will obtain in heaven and earth : "knowledge," likewise, "will become useless," *i.e.*, laborious and imperfect apprehension of truth will be done away, as when you have perfectly acquired a language you leave grammars and primers alone : they have done their work, and you need them no more. This failure is owing to the fragmentary nature of our knowledge, and of our enunciation of that we know; " for we know in part (ἐκ μέρους), and we prophesy in part (ἐκ μέρους, compare Heb. i. 1, πολυμερῶς, *in many fragments*). But when that which is perfect is come then that which is in part shall be done away. When I was a child I spake as a child, I understood as a child, I thought as a child; but when I became a man I put away childish things." Our present imperfection is only introductory to our future and final perfection : as with the words, thoughts, and reasonings of a child, natural and necessary in childhood, and containing the germ of that which is afterward matured in manhood. but in their transitory form childish and unremaining. " For now we see by means of a mirror (δι᾿ ἐσόπτροι, their mirrors were of burnished metal) darkly (ἐν αἰνίγματι, " in a riddle"), but then face to face." The reference is to Numbers xii. 8 (στόμα κατὰ στόμα . . : οὐ δι᾿ αἰνιγμάτων, LXX.), where the Lord contrasts his personal revelations of himself to Moses with visions or dreams. Now we see him in the mirror of his creation, his word, his Church; but then we shall see him face to face. "Now I know in part, but then shall I know even as also I am known." Now our knowledge is fragmentary, and therefore evanescent; but then to its utmost limit (for no finite being can ever obtain omniscience) our knowledge of Christ will resemble Christ's knowledge of us, being perfect, symmetrical, unperplexed, and eternal.

And as with the body and the mind, so likewise with the then perfectly sanctified spirit. We shall be holy, for he is holy. God hath chosen us in Christ before the foundation of the world, that we should be holy Ephes. i. 4. and without blame before him in love: that good pleasure of his goodness will then be fulfilled. He "is able to present us faultless before the presence of his Jude 24. glory with exceeding joy;" and he will accomplish that which his love designs. Of the hundred and forty and four thousand on Mount Zion we read, "They are Rev. xiv. 5. without fault before the throne of God." "Beloved," writes St. John, "now are we the sons of God, and it hath never yet appeared (οὔπω ἐφανερώθη) what we shall be: but we know that when He shall appear (φανερώθῃ, our manifestation being synchronous with his, cf. Col. iii. 4) we shall be like him, because (ὅτι) we 1 John iii. 2. shall see him as he is." Not only will our body be fashioned like unto the body of his glory, and our mind be clear as the light, but then will our spirit drink in, to the utmost limit of the capacity of each, the beams of his eternal love. For then will the prayer of our great High Priest be fulfilled, "Father, I will that they also whom thou hast given me be with me where I am, that they may behold my glory;" and his promise (of which we may safely say heaven has nothing higher) be accomplished, "I will declare unto them thy name, that the love wherewith thou hast loved me may be in them and I in them." We shall see his face, and his name shall be in our foreheads.

John xvii. 24, 26.

Now all this personal perfection of the glorified saints will be the triumphant issue of the Holy Spirit's work upon them and within them. Whatever spiritual faculties and graces they now possess are "the first-fruits of the Spirit;" and the first-fruits are only the pledge of the golden harvest and of the overflowing vintage. The seal wherewith now they are sealed is "the earnest * of the Spirit in their hearts:" the fruition of the inheritance, of which it is an earnest, is yet to come. They are here sowing to the Spirit— often weeping, as they go forth and bear the precious seed—and they shall hereafter, not independently of, or apart from the Spirit, but they shall OF THE SPIRIT (ἐκ τοῦ Πνεύματος) reap life everlasting. Every precious grace, which he has planted and cultivated and cherished in this wintry world, shall bud and blossom and bring forth fruit in that better land of everlasting summer. There the flesh will never lust against the Spirit; nor will the Spirit there need to make intercession for us with groanings which cannot be uttered. For there man's complex being will be one melodious harmony again, and every saint will be a perfectly purified temple of the Holy Ghost.

Rom. viii. 23.

2 Cor. i. 22.

Ephes. i. 14.

Gal. vi. 8.

(2) The issue of the Holy Spirit's work will be seen in the completion of the Elect Church.

Not one saint will be wanting from that heavenly society. "The Son of Man," we read, "will send forth his angels, and they shall gather together his elect from the four winds, from one end of heaven to the other."

Matt. xxiv. 31.

---

* ἀρραβῶν. Heb., *arabh*, "to give in pledge;" something given as present and part payment, and as a pledge of future and full payment.

This will be "our gathering together (ἐπισυναγωγή)

2 Thess. ii. 1. unto him." Then shall the children of God, who are now

John xi. 52. scattered abroad, be gathered together into one. The whole family, which is now part in heaven and part on

Ephes. iii. 15. earth, shall then all meet in the presence of their one Father. Then shall those over whom we have sorrowed, and still sorrow, as sleeping in Jesus, be reunited with us in his presence, and be for ever with us and with the Lord in the full enjoyment of indissoluble com-

1 Thess. iv. munion. All shall meet in the many mansions of the
13—18. Father's house, prepared for them by Christ himself in the holy Jerusalem, the city which hath foundations, whose maker and builder is God.

Then shall Christ present his bride the Church unto himself in glorious beauty, not having spot, or wrinkle, or any such thing, but holy and without blemish before

Ephes. v. 27. him for ever. It is true, that in a subordinate sense every believer even now may say, " I am my Beloved's,

Song vi. 3. and my Beloved is mine ;" and that the spiritual father of every community of believers may re-echo the words of St. Paul regarding the Corinthians, " I have espoused you to one husband, that I may present you as a chaste

2 Cor. xi. 2. virgin to Christ." But for the bridal of the whole Church we wait for the time when the voice shall be heard, "as it were the voice of a great multitude, and as the voice of many waters, and as the voice of mighty thunderings, saying, Alleluia ! for the Lord God omnipotent reigneth. Let us be glad, and rejoice, and give honour to him, for the marriage of the Lamb is come,

Rev. xix. 6, 7. and his wife hath made herself ready." Not till then will the bride be complete.

And if now the Holy Spirit ratifies the union between the soul and Christ, when the door of the heart is opened at the voice of the knocking Saviour, surely it will be the triumph of his Divine and delightful fellowship

when the whole company of the redeemed and glorified
church is called to the marriage-supper of the Lamb. Rev. xix. 9.
Not till then will be understood in the fulness of their
meaning the wonderful words, There is one Body and
one Spirit, even as ye are called in one hope of your
calling. Ephes. iv. 4.

Then shall the spiritual temple be complete. It is
true, that even now it is demanded of each one of us,
" What ! know ye not that your body is the temple of
the Holy Ghost, which is in you, which ye have of
God ?" But, in another and a fuller sense, every believer 1 Cor. vi. 19.
is but one living stone of that building, which is in
process of erection on the heavenly Mount Zion. The
saints are now being builded upon the foundations of
the apostles and prophets, Jesus Christ himself being
the chief corner stone, in whom all the building, fitly
framed together, groweth unto a holy temple in the
Lord. This building is " for an habitation of God
THROUGH THE SPIRIT." And if, on the completion of Ephes. ii. 20
Solomon's temple, we read, " It came even to pass, as —22.
the trumpeters and singers were as one to make one
sound to be heard in praising and thanking the Lord,
and when they lifted up their voice with the trumpets
and cymbals and instruments of music, and praised the
Lord, saying, ' For he is good, for his mercy endureth
for ever,' that then the house was filled with a cloud,
even the house of the Lord, so that the priests could not
stand to minister by reason of the cloud, for the glory
of the Lord had filled the house of God "—if such were 2 Chron. v. 13
the gracious manifestation of God's presence on the 14.
consecration of the material temple, what far more
exceeding glory, and what higher and heavenlier
beatitude, may we not anticipate will fill the courts of
his spiritual habitation for evermore ?

Then shall we have come, not only by anticipative

CHAP. IX.

faith, but in blessed reality, "unto Mount Zion, and unto the city of the living God, the heavenly Jerusalem, and to an innumerable company of angels, to the general assembly and church* of the firstborn which are written in heaven." The muster-roll of the citizens of the heavenly city will then have been read, and not one, whose name is in the book of life, shall be wanting from that festal throng and church of the firstborn. And here the myriads of the angels are united with the multitudes of the redeemed. See the glowing picture of their harmonious adoration as portrayed in the Apocalypse. Will not this be a triumphant issue of the Eternal Spirit's work in the church? If now, amid all the distractions of this fallen world, he can draw forth acceptable worship and thanksgiving from the hearts of his struggling people, so that even here God inhabits the praises of Israel, what will be the effectual energy of his grace in the uninterrupted and melodious songs of glory?

And then shall the Redeemer see of the travail of his soul and be satisfied. He rejoices in the Holy Spirit's work in every one of his children. But different saints catch different rays of light : all indeed feel and confess their ruin by sin, their redemption through his blood, their access through Christ by one Spirit unto the Father—but with this essential unity the shades of spiritual character are well-nigh infinite. Yea, different branches of his church here reflect different aspects of his

Side notes: Heb. xii. 22, 23.   Rev. v. 8—14.   Isa. liii. 11.

---

* The words translated " to the general assembly and church " (πανηγύρει καὶ ἐκκλησίᾳ) are perhaps rather drawn from classical than sacred literature ; the first, which occurs here only in the New Testament, signifying an assembly of the whole nation at some high festival, as that of Greece at the Olympic games ; the second denoting at Athens the legislative assembly of citizens summoned by the crier.

truth, some reflecting one and some another most vividly. Yea more, different ages and generations have elaborated and illustrated different truths of the one everlasting gospel most conspicuously ; it needs but to mention the doctrine of the Trinity in Unity during the first four centuries, that of justification by faith at the Reformation, that of the new birth of the Spirit in the great evangelical revival at the close of the eighteenth century, and that of missionary enterprise in our own. It may be, as many think, that the church of Christ has yet many lessons to learn or re-learn, amid times of trial and persecution, before the second advent of her Lord ; but, be this as it may, when he shall have fulfilled his promise, "If I go and prepare a place for you I will come again and receive you unto myself, that where I am there ye may be also ;" then will he look upon his church and say, "Thou art all fair, my love : there is no spot in thee." The Holy Spirit's education and purification of the Bride shall then be complete ; and the words of the prophet shall find their accomplishment, " The Lord thy God in the midst of thee is mighty : he will save ; he will rejoice over thee with joy ; he will rest in his love ; he will joy over thee with singing." John xiv. 3.

Song iv. 7.

Zeph. iii. 17.

(3) The issue of the Holy Spirit's work will be seen in the new heavens and earth, wherein dwelleth righteousness.

In treating of this inheritance of the saints, I would not conceal the solemn and awful reverse to their joyful immortality which Holy Scripture affirms to be the everlasting portion of the enemies of God. They in their day of probation have resisted the Spirit of grace to the uttermost limit of Divine mercy ; and not the faintest hope is held out that he, being finally repulsed in this world, will ever renew their unregenerate nature in the world to come. No hint is given that such re-

The issue of the Spirit's work

newal is possible. They have not the Spirit of Christ: they are none of his. They will be for ever subdued under the feet of a triumphant Lord; but they will be subdued, not saved. They will be cast out of his pre-
Rev. xx. 15. sence into the lake of fire, which is the second death. And the word of God declares their doom to be irre-
Matt. xxv. versible, and their punishment eternal.
46.

But I am now treating of that inheritance incor- ruptible, undefiled, and unfading, which is reserved for the people of God. And that the earth shall be filled
Hab. ii. 14. with the knowledge of the glory of the Lord as the waters cover the sea; that Christ must reign till he hath put all
1 Cor. xv. 25. enemies under his feet; that if we suffer with him here
2 Tim. ii. 12. we shall reign with him for ever; that in that glorious
Zech. xiv. 9. kingdom there shall be one Lord and his name one; that
Luke xi. 2. his will shall be done as in heaven so on earth; that of the increase of his government and peace there shall be
Isa. ix. 7. no end;—of all these things we are assured on the word of him who cannot lie. In that sinless and boundless kingdom of the Son of God the saints will exercise their "royal priesthood." And then will the opening dox- ology of the book of Revelation be sung in all the plenitude of its meaning, "Unto him that loved us and washed us from our sins in his own blood, and hath made us kings and priests unto God and his Father, to
Rev. i. 5, 6. him be glory and dominion for ever and ever. Amen." We must not hide from ourselves either aspect of the coming glory. The saints will be kings as well as priests. But for both these offices alike they require the holy anointing oil of the Spirit of God. That
John xiv. 16; unction is theirs, and will abide with them for ever.
1 John ii.
27. Then will the Father have "gathered together in one all things in Christ, which are in heaven and which are
Ephes. i. 10. in earth:" then "in the name of Jesus every knee shall bow, of things in heaven, and things on earth, and

things under the earth, and every tongue confess that
Jesus Christ is Lord to the glory of God the Father : "
then shall God " by Christ have reconciled all things
to himself, whether they be things in earth or things
in heaven." This pure and perfect creation shall be
the illimitable field, in which the saints shall fulfil their
blessed and beatific service. Will not this be the final
triumph of the Eternal Spirit's work ? For if he can
and does carry on his Divine operations with such
feeble and imperfect instruments in this world of sin
and sorrow, energizing effectually in his people, and
dividing to every man severally as he wills, what will
be the facility and the glory of his administrations in a
sinless universe ?

And to this the closing vision of the Apocalypse
seems to refer, bringing before us, according to the
symbolic language of that book, the onward and cease-
less flow of the Holy Spirit's living and life-giving
grace. " And he showed me," writes the beloved
apostle, " a pure river of water of life, clear as crystal,
proceeding (ἐκπορευόμενον, cf. John xv. 26) out of the
throne of God and of the Lamb : in the midst of the
street of it, and on either side of the river was there
the tree of life, which bare twelve manner of fruits,
and yielded her fruit every month ; and the leaves of
the tree were for the healing (θεραπείαν, or " service ") of
the nations." Water is the frequent type of the Holy
Spirit in Scripture. And, — whatever be the actual fulfilment of this prophecy in the heavenly Jerusalem, —
as emblems this crystal river of life seems to import
the pure and holy joys of the Eternal Spirit, proceeding
from the Father and the Son ; this fruit, in its successive variety, the ever new and ever enduring
pleasures of immortality ; and the leaves of the tree,
which are for the service of the nations, those tender

Phil. ii. 10, 11

Col. i. 20.

Rev. xxii. 1, 2.
See Isa. xliv.
3 ; John
vii. 37-39,
etc.

ministries of love which will not be wanting in that world of cloudless felicity. In the vision of holy waters vouchsafed to the prophet, we read, " Everything shall live whither the river cometh " — and so doubtless will it be in the flow of this celestial river of the water of life. But as there, when the prophet's guide had measured a thousand cubits and brought him through the waters, the waters were to the ankles ; and when again he measured a thousand and brought him through the waters, the waters were to the knees ; and when again he measured a thousand and brought him through the waters, the waters were to the loins ; but when after that he measured a thousand, we read the waters were risen, waters to swim in, a river that could not be passed over ; so is it in our furthest and loftiest conceptions of the progressive development of the Holy Spirit's work. We can only pause with reverent footstep on the boundary of the infinite and the unknown. We can only re-echo the awestruck Psalmist's words, " Thy way is in the sea, and thy path in the great waters, and thy footsteps are not known." We can only worship with the adoring apostle, and say, O the depth of the riches both of the wisdom and knowledge of God ! how unsearchable are his judgments, and his ways past finding out ! For of him, and through him, and to him are all things, to whom be glory for ever. Amen.

(margin note beside paragraph: Ezek. xlvii. 1-12.)

(margin note beside paragraph: Psa. lxxvii. 19.)